DEFENDING THE CONQUEST

DEFENDING THE CONQUEST

Bernardo de Vargas Machuca's
Defense and Discourse of the Western Conquests

Edited by Kris Lane
Translated by Timothy F. Johnson

The Pennsylvania State University Press
University Park, Pennsylvania

Library of Congress Cataloging-in-Publication Data
Vargas Machuca, Bernardo de, 1557–1622.
[Milicia y descripción de las Indias. English]
   Defending the conquest : Bernardo de Vargas
   Machuca's Defense and discourse of the western
   conquests / edited by Kris Lane ; translated by
   Timothy F. Johnson.
      p.   cm.—(Latin American originals ; 4)
Includes bibliographical references and index.
Summary: "An English translation and critical edi-
tion of a refutation, written about 1603 by the soldier
Bernardo de Vargas Machuca, of Bartolome de las
Casas's famous Brief Account of the Destruction of
the Indies (1558)"—Provided by publisher.
ISBN 978-0-271-02937-5 (pbk. : alk. paper)
1. America—Early works to 1600.
2. Indians of the West Indies—Early works to 1800.
3. Indians of South America—Early works to 1800.
4. Military art and science—America—Early works
to 1800.
5. America—Discovery and exploration—Spanish—
Early works to 1800.
I. Lane, Kris E., 1967– .
II. Johnson, Timothy F.
III. Title.

E141.V313 2010
970.01′6—dc22
                                  2010024251

It is the policy of The Pennsylvania State University
Press to use acid-free paper. Publications on uncoated
stock satisfy the minimum requirements of American
National Standard for Information Sciences—
Permanence of Paper for Printed Library Material,
ANSI Z39.48–1992.

CONTENTS

Latin American Originals (LAO) is a series of primary source texts on colonial and nineteenth-century Latin America. LAO volumes are accessible, affordable editions of texts translated into English—most of them for the very first time, as is the case with *Defending the Conquest* (LAO 4). The first half-dozen books in the series illuminate aspects of the Spanish conquests during the long century of 1494–1613.

Taken in the chronological order of their primary texts, LAO 5 comes first. *Of Cannibals and Kings* will present the very first written attempt to describe the native cultures of the Americas. This early ethnography, written by a Catalan but surviving only in Italian, is packaged with complementary Spanish texts and placed within the context of the conquest and collapse of the complex societies of the Caribbean islands in the late 1490s. *Invading Guatemala* (LAO 2) shows how reading multiple accounts of conquest wars (in this case, Spanish, Nahua, and Maya versions of the Guatemalan conflict of the 1520s) can explode established narratives and suggest a conquest story that is more complicated, disturbing, and revealing. *Invading Colombia*, the first book in the LAO series, challenges us to view the difficult Spanish invasion of Colombia in the 1530s as more representative of conquest campaigns than the better-known assaults on the Mexica and Inca empires. *Forgotten Franciscans* (LAO 6) will cast light on the spiritual conquest and the conflictive cultural world of the Inquisition in sixteenth-century Mexico. *The Conquest on Trial* (LAO 3) features a fictional embassy of native Americans filing a complaint over the conquest in a Spanish court—the Court of Death. That text, the first theatrical examination of the conquest published in Spain, effectively condensed contemporary debates on colonization into one dramatic package. It reminds us that Bartolomé de las Casas was not the only Spaniard to question the motives and methods of the conquistadors.

The text presented here in *Defending the Conquest* is a self-declared response to—and denunciation of—Las Casas. It was written by a little-known veteran conquistador named Captain don Bernardo de Vargas Machuca, who submitted it unsuccessfully for publication in 1613. Vargas Machuca's spirited and polemic apologia for the Spanish conquest did not see print until 1879 (and in English, not until now). One might imagine that the conquistador would be grateful for the attention that his essay has now been given. But Vargas Machuca was unswervingly cantankerous. Were he alive today, Kris Lane and Timothy Johnson have observed with appropriately wry humor, "he would probably hunt us down and kill us."

The source texts to LAO volumes are either archival documents—written in Spanish, Portuguese, or indigenous languages such as Nahuatl, Zapotec, and Maya—or they are rare books published in the colonial period in their original languages (Spanish, Portuguese, Italian, Latin). The contributing authors are historians, anthropologists, art historians, and scholars of literature; they have developed a specialized knowledge that allows them to locate, translate, and present these texts in a way that contributes to scholars' understanding of the period while also making them readable for students and nonspecialists.

Lane and Johnson are scholars of such a caliber. Lane teaches at the College of William & Mary and is an internationally recognized leading historian of early Latin America. He has published widely acclaimed books on piracy, on Ecuador, and on emerald mining and trading, all focused on the sixteenth and seventeenth centuries. Few scholars active today have as profound and well-informed an understanding of the Spanish conquest, especially in the northern regions of South America (today's Ecuador, Panama, Colombia, and Venezuela). Those regions were the world in which Vargas Machuca pursued his career in "the Indies," and Lane has now become the world's leading expert on this conquistador-author. In addition to the manuscript presented here, Lane and Johnson—who teaches at the University of California and has acquired a masterly understanding of Vargas Machuca's Spanish prose—also recently published the first English edition of the conquistador's lengthy manual for fighting "Indians," his *Milicia indiana*. Whether Vargas Machuca himself would have liked it or not, his provocative, cranky, often offensive, sometimes brilliant, sometimes absurd perspectives on the Spanish conquest are about to be read and discussed far more than they were in his own day. As indeed they deserve to be.

—Matthew Restall

The Spanish conquest of the Americas ranks among the great watersheds in global history. It is also among the most frequently misrepresented. Unlike many such violent episodes, what soldier Bernardo de Vargas Machuca termed Spain's "western conquests" constituted a long and unfinished sequence of events carried out almost entirely by private parties driven by local and personal rather than imperial goals. Despite some astonishing moments, such as Francisco Pizarro's capture of the Inca Atawallpa in Cajamarca, Peru, in 1532, the conquest was neither quick nor the product of regular, pitched battles. Neither was it intentionally genocidal, even if it had that effect in many places. Although they plundered temples and tombs, stole lands, slew warriors, and raped maidens, the Spaniards' main goal was to collect tribute-paying subjects and watch them multiply. The majority of armed actors were not even Spaniards or other Europeans, but rather indigenous peoples who allied with the victorious invaders for a variety of reasons, not all of them far-sighted. Enslaved Africans and free people of color also participated in many successful and unsuccessful expeditions, and some won freedom and other rewards. Conquest, even when it failed, was a shared project.

It was, however, the Spanish invaders and their monarchs who were individually and collectively responsible for the conquest's ways, means, direction, and aftermath. Although indigenous allies and conquered peoples forced many compromises and adjustments, most were treated as permanently inferior wards, made to extract precious minerals, grow cash crops, tend livestock, do laundry and other household chores, and otherwise provide their conquerors with income and personal service. Frontier "rebels" were sometimes enslaved, branded, and sold, but even the vast majority of native Americans who were not so treated, including conquest allies, had to live with far less dignity than Spanish peasants, their closest legal equivalent.

It is also often forgotten that the conquistadors themselves faced quick and ignominious demotions. Spain's kings sought to nip these freelance fighting men's noble pretensions in the bud, fearing (as they had reason to in Spain) the formation of a politically powerful bloc. The answer was bureaucrats. Anxious to do the king's bidding and advance their own careers, university-trained bureaucrats followed close on the heels of the conquerors to set up complex structures of governance and revenue collection. These Spanish *letrados* proved quick studies in overseas empire building, and by as early as 1600 they had accomplished what one historian has labeled a "conquest after the conquest."[1] Conquistador descendants bickered for generations, but to no avail. Military conquest, meanwhile, carried on uninterrupted at the jungle and desert fringes until Spanish American independence in the nineteenth century. Headed by generation after generation of frontier settlers, this endless project of "Indian fighting" was always aided by newfound indigenous, *mestizo*, and African-descended allies.

How could all this conquest and empire building in native American territories be justified? In short, by faith. In 1493, just one year after Columbus's fateful first voyage, Pope Alexander VI, himself a Spaniard, granted Spain exclusive rights to trade and plunder beyond an imaginary line 370 leagues west of the Cape Verde Islands in exchange for the promise to spread the Catholic faith. Although many Spanish subjects used the pope's grant as a license to murder and steal, others took seriously the command to propagate the faith. Even Columbus, who at first proposed enslavement of native peoples, was persuaded by Queen Isabella to employ gentler means of subjection and to sponsor Hieronymite missionaries. The feudal-style *encomienda* system of allotting indigenous peoples to grandees slowly took shape, but missionaries soon saw their projects annulled as indigenous wards died from abuse and disease. Unable to rein in gold-hungry colonists, Columbus sailed off in search of the Great Khan. The early missionaries gave up or searched in vain for utopian enclaves free of settlers.

---

1. Peter Bakewell, "Conquest After the Conquest: The Rise of Spanish Domination in America," in Richard Kagan and Geoffrey Parker, eds., *Spain, Europe, and the Atlantic World: Essays in Honour of John H. Elliott* (New York: Cambridge University Press, 1995), 296–315.

Into this troubled milieu came Bartolomé de las Casas, an encomienda holder's son from Seville who himself briefly became an *encomendero* on Hispaniola. The experience sparked a Paul-like conversion: within a few years, Las Casas became a priest, and then a lifelong defender of all Amerindians against abuses perpetrated by his countrymen. A close confidant of Spain's young Habsburg king, Charles I (Holy Roman Emperor Charles V after 1518), Las Casas managed to have even encomiendas sharply curbed—all this during or immediately after the conquests of Mexico, Guatemala, Peru, and Colombia. Not only the conquistadors, who came to regard the friar as at best a liar and at worst a traitor, objected to Las Casas's outspoken efforts to defend native peoples in the name of the faith. Many high-ranking theologians, as well as numerous missionaries in the Americas, also disagreed vehemently with Las Casas's moral and legal claims, some arguing in favor of Amerindian slavery, others for permanent title to encomiendas.

While native Americans were not asked their opinion, Spanish churchmen such as Las Casas and Juan Ginés de Sepúlveda debated the justice of conquest at the king's request in the 1540s and 1550s. Las Casas argued that native peoples, despite some misguided acts of violence, were innocent, tractable pagans who had violated no laws, and thus the pope's decree was to be read as a call for peaceful conversion by unarmed missionaries. Sepúlveda argued that native peoples (with whom he had no significant contact, having never gone to the Americas) had broken laws against nature itself, engaging in cannibalism, human sacrifice, infanticide, sodomy, and other acts impeding human procreation. War against such "unnaturally inclined" peoples was justified, he argued, both as punishment for these crimes (along with "sins" such as idolatry) and for protection of the innocent.

Also left out of the debate were the conquistadors. Both Pizarro and Cortés were dead by the time Las Casas formally confronted Sepúlveda in 1550–51, but some cranky survivors offered their mostly unheard opinions well into the 1570s. Later arrivals, cut out of the conquest of empires and scramble for encomiendas, felt even more slighted. Wide dissemination of Las Casas's inflammatory writings beyond the Spanish world only rubbed salt in their wounds. Most such luckless and angry conquistadors got themselves killed or maimed in frontier skirmishes, but not all could be silenced or ignored. One such man, Bernardo de Vargas Machuca of Simancas, offered a rare "conquistador response" to Las Casas. First penned about 1603 in Portobelo, Panama, he called it *Defense of the Western Conquests,* or *Apologetic Discourses.* Despite the fact that Las Casas had been dead for some forty years, royal censors denied publication of Vargas Machuca's counterpolemical tract. It remained an orphan of the archives until it was rediscovered and published in Spanish along with many other "lost" colonial manuscripts in 1879. The present translation is based on one of two surviving manuscript copies of Vargas Machuca's tract, dated 1618, now housed in the University of Salamanca library.

We thank Franklin Knight, Brett Rushforth, Paul Mapp, Samuel G. Armistead, Valerie Billing, Matthew Zealand, Manuel Gómez Navarro, and an anonymous reader for their valuable comments on the first draft manuscript, and Felipe Fernández-Armesto for his incisive and thoughtful reading of the introduction. We are likewise indebted to Hiroshi Kitamura for help with a Japanese edition of Vargas Machuca, and to Laura Reed-Morrisson, Patty Mitchell, and Kathryn Yahner at Penn State University Press for their patience and editorial expertise. Remaining errors should be blamed on us. Last, we thank editor Sandy Thatcher and series editors Matthew Restall and J. Michael Francis for inviting our submission and then seeing it through to production.

We hold as a thing most certain and true that in these forty

years there have been above twelve million souls—men, women,

and children—killed, tyrannically and unjustly, on account of the

tyrannical actions and infernal works of Christians; and in truth

I do believe, without thinking to deceive myself, that they were

above fifteen million.

—Fray Bartolomé de las Casas

Introduction to Bernardo de Vargas Machuca's *Defense of the Western Conquests*, or *Apologetic Discourses*

KRIS LANE

To pick a fight with a dead man may not be the height of valor, but as any scholar knows, one can still lose. The Spanish-born soldier and writer of military manuals Bernardo de Vargas Machuca (ca. 1555–1622) was nothing if not bold to grapple with Fray Bartolomé de las Casas (1484–1566), even if his opponent had been dead for nearly half a century. Las Casas was a famously fierce critic of the conquistadors for much of his long life, and his voluminous writings and personal legacy of pro-indigenous activism remained formidable in the Spanish world and beyond long after his death. Las Casas was never sainted, but intellectually and morally he remained a hard target even in 1613, when Vargas Machuca first submitted his manuscript to Spanish censors.

Others had tried to counter Las Casas in his lifetime, among them top theologians and conquest-hardened soldiers, but at Spain's Habsburg court Las Casas always won hearts, if not minds. For conquistadors, this was where it mattered; kings such as Charles V (r. 1516–56) and his son, Philip II (r. 1556–98), issued the relevant decrees and doled out or withheld rewards. The kings' wives, daughters, and mothers were similarly moved by priestly appeals to royal piety and were influential in shaping colonial policy. Even Hernán Cortés struggled for recognition despite having brought down the Aztec state, and his followers found that rewards came much harder. After 1542, the king stripped customary titles and sinecures from the conquerors throughout the colonies as a result of laws pushed through by Las Casas. The so-called New Laws provoked such violent reactions, especially in Peru, that they diminished the friar's power at court.

Were America's native peoples well served by Las Casas's tireless reformism? Only partially: serious abuses were more often reported and sometimes prosecuted as a result of the friar's efforts, but royal concessions, including new and extended encomiendas in frontier areas, continued despite the New Laws. Enormous distances, coupled with a hardy Castilian tradition of frontier paramilitary raiding (codified by Vargas Machuca in his 1599 manual, *The Indian Militia*), proved powerful enemies of early Habsburg attempts at benevolent absolutism. The crown's ballooning budgetary demands were even more corrosive of pro-indigenous policies. As a result of these factors, conditions on the ground in the colonies remained but a dim reflection of royal mandates throughout the sixteenth century, a situation exacerbated by the 1598 death of Philip II. The Prudent King's increasingly weak successors expressed sympathy for indigenous subjects abroad, but did little of substance to help them.

How did native Americans fare in places where the friars had outmaneuvered the conquistadors? Spanish America's many frontier missions offered some physical security (despite an elevated risk of death by disease), but Spain's inquisitorial Church Militant, as Vargas Machuca bitingly observes in his *Defense* below, was not known for its light touch. Ample evidence suggests that many native Americans happily embraced Christianity as presented by early Catholic missionaries, yet there is also much evidence confirming that more than a few willful congregants suffered severe beatings, exile, and in some cases execution for alleged acts of apostasy or heresy. Although an outspoken opponent of such harsh measures, Las Casas was more a lobbyist than a missionary. It was in 1516, well before the mainland American conquests, that Spain's Cardinal Jiménez de Cisneros named Las Casas "Protector of the Indians." Las Casas attempted to live up to the challenge of this title by playing the role of public advocate rather than mission director (or even bishop, his next title), but in the end he was forced to admit that his work had been insufficient to stave off disaster.

If he had largely failed, then, in his efforts to "protect" the Indians, Las Casas had certainly *not* failed to harm the *indianos*, or "India men," like the conquistadors and their descendants and imitators. Indeed, what motivated Vargas Machuca to take on Las Casas in the

first decades of the seventeenth century was the gut-level outrage
of an aging Indies hand who had arrived too late to conquer his own
Mexico or Peru—and whose minor but near-fatal exploits in the
jungles of Colombia went unrewarded thanks to (he felt) Las Casas's
false testimony before past kings. Vargas Machuca believed that he
had no choice but to defend the conquistadors' honor against rank
defamation.

Distant monarchs had been misled, Vargas Machuca claimed, and
Las Casas's *Account, Much Abbreviated, of the Destruction of the
Indies* (best known in Spanish as the *Brevísima relación*, circulated in
manuscript after 1542 and published in 1552), more than any other
piece of writing, had turned Spain's monarchs against the conquistadors.[1] Now that a new king, Philip III (1598–1621), was on the
throne, Vargas Machuca sought to offer his corrections. Somewhat
like Cortés's unacknowledged companion Bernal Díaz del Castillo,
author of the *True History of the Conquest of New Spain* (composed
after 1568), Vargas Machuca cast himself as a seasoned and dispas-
sionate yet deeply pious participant-observer, a practical military
man.[2] Years of experience and a detached reappraisal of "the facts," he
believed, were enough to demolish Las Casas's exaggerated claims of
abuse. He would do so not simply for the sake of righting the historical record, however; like Bernal Díaz, he expected to be personally
rewarded. Such was the culture of *mercedes*.

As in so many other things in his life, Vargas Machuca's tim-
ing was off. Young Philip III may have been less interested in the

1. In English, we have relied on the following edition: Bartolomé de las Casas,
An Account, Much Abbreviated, of the Destruction of the Indies, ed. Franklin Knight,
trans. Andrew Hurley (Indianapolis: Hackett, 2003). The literature on Las Casas is
vast and growing; interested readers may wish to visit www.lascasas.org, and teachers
should consult the essays in *Approaches to Teaching the Writings of Bartolomé de Las
Casas*, ed. Santa Arias and Eyda Merediz (New York: Modern Language Association,
2008).

2. See Davíd Carrasco's fine critical edition of Bernal Díaz del Castillo's *The
History of the Conquest of New Spain* (Albuquerque: University of New Mexico
Press, 2008). See also Arthur P. Stabler and John E. Kicza, "Ruy González's 1553 Letter
to Emperor Charles V: An Annotated Translation," *The Americas* 42:4 (April 1986):
473–87. González, a councilman in the Mexican capital, put his opinion bluntly: "Your
Majesty ought not to permit Father Friar Bartholomew thus to vilify your vassals"
(481). As for native Mexicans, González had this to say: "these people were barbarous,
idolatrous, sacrificers and killers of innocent people, eaters of human flesh, most filthy
and nefarious sodomites" (485).

welfare of indigenous Americans than his father and grandfather had been, but the tide had still not turned in favor of their conquerors.[3] Las Casas's influence was still so strong in Spain that when Vargas Machuca submitted his point-by-point *Defense* in 1613, it was not allowed to be published despite the support of notable Dominicans. With still more reason to hate Las Casas, Vargas Machuca died in Madrid seeking the ear of yet another young king, Philip IV, in 1622. By Philip IV's time there was a move afoot to ban publication of the long-dead Dominican preacher's works, but the pendulum soon swung back. The king's second wife, Mariana of Austria, partly rekindled the spirit of Las Casas during her regency (1665–75) and the rule of her feeble son, Charles II (1675–1700), last of the Spanish Habsburgs. After the Bourbon succession in 1700, the unbridled cruelty of the "ancient conquistadors" went virtually undisputed. At independence, Simón Bolívar reaffirmed the "truth" of Las Casas's accusations in his Jamaica Letter of 1815, as they proved useful to the cause of freedom from "tyrant Spain."[4]

The Opponent

The Seville-born Dominican Bartolomé de las Casas was one of the most influential writers of the sixteenth century. His famous 1552 denunciation of the conquistadors, the *Very Brief Account of*

3. Benjamin Keen marked the turn as follows: "To be sure, the immense prestige of Las Casas served for a time to prevent the publication of such attacks upon him as that of Captain Vargas Machuca, who claimed that a 'Huguenot translation' of the *Very Brief Account of the Destruction of the Indies,* Las Casas's exposé of Spanish cruelties in the New World, spread lies about Spain and her work in the Indies. That prestige, joined to the very strength of Las Casas's theological-juridical doctrines, no doubt also contributed to the denial of publication for Sarmiento de Gamboa's [1572] anti-Lascasian history of Peru, commissioned by Viceroy Toledo. But these small mercies could not conceal the fact that the Lascasian reform project was dead." See Keen's introduction to Juan Friede and Benjamin Keen, eds., *Bartolomé de las Casas in History: Toward an Understanding of the Man and His Work* (DeKalb: Northern Illinois University Press, 1971), 6. See also Pedro Sarmiento de Gamboa, *History of the Incas,* trans. and ed. Brian S. Bauer and Vania Smith (Austin: University of Texas Press, 2007). A far less rabid opponent of Las Casas than Vargas Machuca, Sarmiento has this to say about the friar: "Although his zeal seems holy and understandable, he said things about the dominions of this land and against its conquerors that are not supported by the evidence" (40).

4. David Bushnell, ed., *El Libertador: Writings of Simón Bolívar,* trans. Frederick Fornoff (New York: Oxford University Press, 2003), 13.

the Destruction of the Indies, reset the course of colonial policy for centuries afterward and greatly influenced the acts and attitudes of the rest of Europe toward Spain. Within a few decades the book was translated into English, French, Flemish, Dutch, Italian, German, and Latin and was frequently held up as confessional evidence of Spanish tyranny and hypocrisy.

With vivid imagery and an activist's outrage, Las Casas exposed an otherwise hidden world of atrocities on the far side of the Ocean Sea. These were not the cannibal outrages perpetrated by the misnamed "Indians" described by Columbus and Vespucci, but rather the atrocities of fellow Europeans, baptized Catholics run amok in an Edenic New World. Las Casas was a highly learned man, but what gave him the greatest clout among his wide readership was the fact that he had "been there." He was not only an eyewitness but also an encomendero's son who had rubbed elbows with the Columbuses.[5]

Arriving on Hispaniola in 1502, Las Casas witnessed firsthand the mass theft, rape, enslavement, and murder perpetrated by his countrymen. Indigenous women were driven to kill their infant children and commit mass suicide. Chastened, Las Casas went to Spain in 1506 to join the priesthood, was apparently ordained in Rome in 1507, and returned to the Caribbean to serve as chaplain in the bloody 1514 conquest of Cuba. More terrorized than ever by what he saw, Las Casas returned to Spain to become a lifelong promoter of indigenous rights (within his paternalistic missionary sense of them) and a serial denouncer of conquistadors. Not all of his ideas were humane. As early as 1516 he proposed to King Ferdinand relieving indigenous workers by importing more enslaved Africans, a position he later regretted and rejected.[6]

Las Casas did not witness the dramatic conquests of Mexico (1519–21) and Peru (1532–36), but he avidly devoured all available information about them, from written accounts to oral testimonies,

---

5. This much-abbreviated biography is drawn from Lewis Hanke, *Bartolomé de las Casas: An Interpretation of His Life and Writings* (The Hague: Martinus Nijhoff, 1951), and Hanke, *The Spanish Struggle for Justice in the Conquest of America* (Philadelphia: University of Pennsylvania Press, 1949).

6. This point is most clearly and succinctly made by Rolena Adorno in *The Polemics of Possession in Spanish American Narrative* (New Haven: Yale University Press), 64–69. Claims that Las Casas was personally responsible for Africans being brought to the Spanish Indies in the first place are preposterous, as this traffic was well under way prior to his writing.

and with this evidence he began to compose his own multivolume *History of the Indies*. It was a far less polemical work than his famous *Brevísima relación* but one that still emphasized Spanish cruelty and innate indigenous generosity and goodness. Las Casas went much further in this direction by writing a parallel *Apologetic History*, in which he claimed that some Amerindian civilizations were superior to those of the ancient Greeks and Romans—a hard pill to swallow in Renaissance Spain.[7] In this regard, the friar was consistent: indigenous "barbarism," even when violent, was innocent. Spanish barbarity was not.

After joining the Dominican Order in 1522, Las Casas regarded the "excesses" of the conquistadors as more than individual acts of lust or cruelty; they extended to the whole Spanish colonial project. The conquistadors' core aims, he asserted, were the unjust usurpation and plunder of the native lords's households, lands, and subjects—all under the guise of extending the Spanish and Catholic realms for king and pope. Mass enslavement, though already outlawed in 1512, was the de facto result of conquest. Las Casas argued successfully in the early 1540s that the quasi-feudal encomienda, or trusteeship, established under Queen Isabella was really just slavery by another name.

What did Las Casas really want, or expect, to achieve? As a priest working for one of Spain's most powerful mendicant orders, Las Casas was only tangentially interested in charging fellow Spaniards with crimes so that they might be tried and punished. He was not the equivalent of a modern human rights lawyer or activist judge despite his tremendous legal knowledge and special title. Although his views and expectations changed over time, Las Casas's initial goal was to secure exclusive missionary access to the native peoples of the Americas. Lay Spaniards ought to be kept out, he warned Charles V and later Philip II—banned entirely from the hemisphere. Even among priests, none but the most devoted and upright ought to live among what he repeatedly described as innocent and easily misled children of nature.

7. Edited by Agustín Millares Carlo, Las Casas's *Historia de las Indias* was only published in 1951 (Mexico City: FCE, 1951); see also Lewis Hanke, *Bartolomé de las Casas, Historian: An Essay in Spanish Historiography* (Gainesville: University of Florida Press, 1952); and Las Casas, *Apologética historia sumaria*, ed. Edmundo O'Gorman, 2 vols. (Mexico City: UNAM, 1967).

According to Las Casas, God had led the Spaniards to the native peoples of the Americas for one reason: to introduce them to the Catholic Faith. In abusing, exploiting, and killing them under cover of a papal charter, the newcomers had all but sold their souls to the devil. Aside from his constant calls to suspend "discovery" licenses, or *capitulaciones,* such as the one that allowed Francisco Pizarro and his brothers to unjustly topple the Inca Empire, Las Casas proposed several utopian schemes. A very early try at mixing Spanish peasants with former indigenous slaves on the Venezuelan coast failed just as the conquest of Mexico was taking place (1519–21). Thanks to reluctant settlers, unstoppable Spanish slavers, and indigenous resistance and flight, the colony never even got started. Although Vargas Machuca claims below that this project was doomed to fail because it was planted in the heart of cannibal country, surviving letters and other evidence suggest that it was simply a stillborn enterprise, with perhaps Las Casas's divided energies, as much as anything else, to blame.[8]

A genuine experimental colony called La Vera Paz, or "True Peace," founded in Guatemala just north of Santiago in 1537, also struggled and was finally abandoned following indigenous uprisings in 1556. Again, the extent of Las Casas's responsibility for the failure is uncertain, but he claimed its early years of joyous baptisms and indigenous-language Christian song as a resounding success.[9] It was here in Guatemala that he received the title of Bishop of Chiapa (today Chiapas, Mexico), but rather than stay and tend to his flock, Las Casas kept traveling back to Spain to press the king for an end to the encomienda. He does not appear to have learned Nahuatl, the Mexican lingua franca, nor any of the Maya dialects spoken in his jurisdiction. A recent critic, Daniel Castro, has suggested that Las Casas never really had the welfare of Amerindians in mind—at least not in any modern sense of the term. He hardly knew them, after all,

8. The Venezuelan project is most fully examined by Marcel Bataillon in his essay, "The *Clérigo* Casas, Colonist and Colonial Reformer," in Friede and Keen, *Bartolomé de las Casas in History,* 353–440. See also Adorno's brief assessment in *The Polemics of Possession,* 72–73.

9. The most thorough examination of this project is Benno M. Biermann's essay, "Bartolomé de las Casas and Verapaz," in Friede and Keen, *Bartolomé de las Casas in History,* 443–84.

and his failed paternalist utopias only show that he was an imperialist of another sort, "another face of empire."[10]

Few empires or emperors, however, have suffered such an outspoken critic as Las Casas. After securing the anti-encomienda New Laws of 1542–43, Las Casas turned his attention to a highly publicized debate in Valladolid (near Vargas Machuca's birthplace of Simancas) that lasted from 1550–51. Although the debate was a serial hearing before a body of judges rather than a one-on-one showdown, the friar's main opponent was the humanist scholar and chronicler Juan Ginés de Sepúlveda (1490–1573), whose somewhat turgid, twelve-point response to Las Casas at Valladolid was "recycled" by Vargas Machuca as a preface (see below). Sepúlveda's 1545 dialogue, *Demócrates segundo* (composed in Latin under the title *Democrates alter*), was a widely read and much-discussed defense of the Spanish conquest wars.[11] Sepúlveda had argued that native Americans could be warred upon for violations of natural law, including human sacrifice, and that in a sense their "natural barbarity," a result of their long isolation, warranted enslavement as a means to achieve acculturation and conversion.

Sepúlveda's argument fell short of embracing Aristotle's theory of natural slavery (roughly, "some humans have strong bodies but weak minds and must therefore be enslaved for the utility of those born to be masters and for their own protection"), but it came close.[12] The point of Valladolid, as Rolena Adorno has argued, was defining "just war," Aristotle's other pretext for enslavement, not debating indigenous humanity. The debate was inconclusive in that no formal winner was declared, but Charles V was persuaded to suspend new conquest petitions briefly. Conquistador rebellions had, however, begun to erode Las Casas's influence at court by 1551, and perhaps it

10. Daniel Castro, *Another Face of Empire: Bartolomé de las Casas, Indigenous Rights, and Ecclesiastical Imperialism* (Durham: Duke University Press, 2007). Castro echoes an earlier and much fiercer detractor, the Spanish historian José Pérez de Barradas, whose 1948 book *Los mestizos de América* cited Vargas Machuca as an authoritative source.

11. Ángel Losada broke down Sepúlveda's key arguments in his essay, "The Controversy Between Sepúlveda and Las Casas in the Junta of Valladolid," in Friede and Keen, *Bartolomé de las Casas in History*, 279–306.

12. For early Spanish discussion of Aristotle's natural slavery theory, including a near-verbatim application of it to native Americans ca. 1600, see Anthony Pagden, *The Fall of Natural Man: The American Indian and the Origins of Comparative Ethnology* (New York: Cambridge University Press, 1982), 44–47.

Map 1 Sixteenth-century Spanish America (Stuart E. Hamilton)

was for this reason that he addressed the 1552 *Brevísima relación* to the future Philip II while he was still a young prince, with the request that he plead the Amerindians' case before his father, Charles V.

As Rolena Adorno has demonstrated, not long before his death in 1566 Las Casas grew even more radical in his critique of the Spanish enterprise in the Indies. By 1562 he was openly arguing that the whole colonial project was unjustifiable and a grave mistake. The Spanish crown, he said, ought to return governance of the Indies to their native lords, the "Indians." After years of failed compromises and experimental colonies, Las Casas had come to believe that both God and Mammon could not be served in the Americas, and that by natural right the land and its products belonged to the native inhabitants regardless of their "infidelity." No wars against them had been just. As Adorno argues, Las Casas's final position was shared by indigenous critics of colonialism writing about the same time as Vargas Machuca, most notably the Peruvian polemicist Guaman Poma de Ayala.[13]

Las Casas's *Very Brief Account of the Destruction of the Indies*

The book that drove Vargas Machuca to take up the language of the duel and challenge a dead priest was essentially a pamphlet, a propaganda piece. Published in Seville just after the Valladolid debate, the *Very Brief Account* or *Brevísima relación* was—and remains—an oddity of Spanish literature. In its day, some took it as a heartfelt and honest report, while others saw only a hard swipe at Sepúlveda that simultaneously clobbered Spain, the king, and the conquistadors (it had in fact been composed in the early 1540s, well before the dispute with Sepúlveda began). Whether they loved it or loathed it, highly educated Spanish readers understood that Las Casas's *Very Brief Account* was intended as a polemic, a persuasive epistle.[14]

But there was also subtle cleverness in the *Brevísima relación*. By calling it an abridgment, Las Casas threw a jab at long-winded Indies chroniclers and historians—those like his enemies Gonzalo Fernández de Oviedo and Francisco López de Gómara, who would elevate

13. Adorno, *The Polemics of Possession*, especially chapter 1.
14. On reception of Las Casas's arguments in learned circles, see Pagden, *Fall of Natural Man*, 108.

Spanish conquests and conquerors as Livy and others had celebrated Rome's—yet he himself was one of them.[15] Las Casas demonstrated elsewhere that he knew the "true" history of the Spanish Empire in America was hardly so simple as his *Very Brief Account* implied, but here the argument, in order to get results from powerful people with short attention spans, demanded the genre. In the long version, the *Apologetic History*, which he read verbatim before the judges at Valladolid, his already mind-numbing list of atrocities went on *ad nauseam*.

Like a twist on the venerable travel itinerary, too, the *Brevísima relación* followed the conquistadors around the Americas, from the Caribbean islands Las Casas knew so well to his beloved Mexico and Central America, and then to the more distant lands of New Granada and Peru, which he never visited (he had been headed to Peru just after the conquest of the Incas in the 1530s, but ended up in Guatemala via Nicaragua). Despite his brevity, Las Casas even managed to squeeze in the River Plate District, Venezuela's Pearl Coast, and Greater Florida. He seemed to want to leave no instance of conquistador shame unexposed in what he called that "hell that is the Indies." The abortive conquest of Chile was left out only because it was still under way as he wrote.

For each of these places, the friar launches immediately into a jaw-dropping sequence of Spanish atrocities (including cannibalism) perpetrated against native inhabitants, his nameless conquistadors "sorry tyrants" who practiced "cruelty without precedent." It is an exposé, but why the repetition and the graphically violent imagery? As a member of the Order of Preachers, Las Casas in his *Very Brief Account* is in full, reiterative preacher mode. Though presented as an epistolary plea to Prince Philip, the tract is a thundering sermon. Like most conquistadors and other nontheologians, Bernardo de Vargas Machuca did not read the *Brevísima relación* as a sermon or propagandistic tract, but rather as a series of barefaced lies masquerading as truth. He took it literally.

15. For a study with portions of text in translation, see Kathleen Ann Myers, *Gonzalo Fernández de Oviedo's Chronicle of America: A New History for a New World*, trans. Nina M. Scott (Austin: University of Texas Press, 2007), and Lesley Bird Simpson, ed. and trans., *Cortés: The Life of the Conqueror by His Secretary, Francisco López de Gómara* (Berkeley: University of California Press, 1965). The original texts were published in 1535 and 1552, respectively.

Bernardo de Vargas Machuca in the Americas

Bernardo de Vargas Machuca was not a conquistador in the usual
sense of the term. Born in the Old Castilian village of Simancas
outside Valladolid about 1555, he was more than a generation behind
Cortés (d. 1547) and Pizarro (d. 1541).[16] By the time Vargas Machuca
reached the West Indies in 1578, the English corsair Francis Drake
was already a well-known menace to Spanish shipping, and it was
the defense of Catholic America against Elizabethan "heretics,"
not native rebels or idolaters, that justified his first trip across the
Atlantic. Prior to his anti-pirate service, which yielded no results,
Vargas Machuca had served as a page for his father in the Alpujarras
Morisco uprising of 1568–71 and afterwards as a low-ranking soldier
in the militias of Spanish Italy.

Records for the years 1579–83 are equivocal, but from various
service reports it appears that Vargas Machuca participated in campaigns to suppress runaway slaves in Panama and rebel Amerindians
in northwest Argentina. Although some scholars have suggested
that he fought the famously rebellious Mapuche or Araucanians in
Chile during this time, there is no evidence of it in any of his various
service reports. In the section on Chile near the end of the *Defense of
the Western Conquests*, and in a 1599 plan he submitted to Spain's
Indies Council on how to conquer the Mapuche with crack teams of
militiamen, he does not claim to have ever been there.

By 1584 Vargas Machuca's path is clearer. He moved to the highlands of New Granada, just north of Bogotá, married a descendant
of a local conquistador, and began to take part in an almost constant stream of pacification campaigns that lasted a decade. He was
recruited by Governor Antonio de Berrío to search for El Dorado in
the neighboring Venezuelan Llanos and Guyana Highlands in 1585
and 1587, but thanks to delays in those expeditions, he ended up
fighting elsewhere in what is today Colombia. (Berrío famously met
up with Walter Raleigh, who captured him on Trinidad in 1595.)

Most of Vargas Machuca's battles and skirmishes took place
among the Muzos and Carares, small Carib-speaking ethnic

16. For a more thorough account of Vargas Machuca's life, see *The Indian Militia
and Description of the Indies* (Durham: Duke University Press, 2008), and María Luisa
Martínez de Salinas, *Castilla ante el Nuevo Mundo: La trayectoría indiana del gobernador Bernardo de Vargas Machuca* (Valladolid, Spain: Diputación Provincial, 1991).

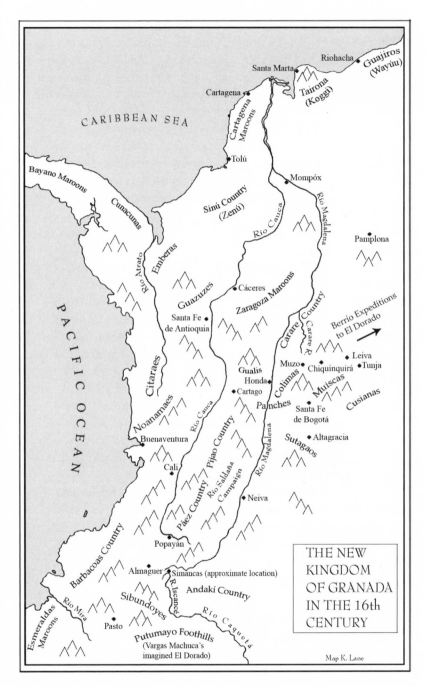

The following labels appear on the map:

CARIBBEAN SEA

PACIFIC OCEAN

Riohacha
Guajiros (Wayúu)
Santa Marta
Tairona (Kogi)
Cartagena
Cartagena Maroons
Bayano Maroons
Tolú
Mompóx
Río Magdalena
Pamplona
Cunacunas
Sinú Country (Zenú)
Río Cauca
Río Atrato
Emberas
Cáceres
Zaragoza Maroons
Guazuzes
Carare Country
Carare R.
Berrío Expeditions to El Dorado
Santa Fe de Antioquia
Citaraes
Leiva
Tunja
Muzo
Chiquinquirá
Gualis
Colimas
Muiscas
Honda
Cartago
Cusianas
Noanamaes
Río Cauca
Panches
Santa Fe de Bogotá
Buenaventura
Pijao Country
Sutagaos
Altagracia
Cali
Río Saldaña Campaign
Páez Country
Río Magdalena
Neiva
Popayán
Barbacoas Country
Almaguer
Simancas (approximate location)
Andakí Country
Sibundoyes
R. Iscancé
Río Mira
Río Caquetá
Esmeraldas Maroons
Pasto
Putumayo Foothills
(Vargas Machuca's imagined El Dorado)

THE NEW KINGDOM OF GRANADA IN THE 16th CENTURY

Map K. Lane

Map 2 New Granada in Vargas Machuca's era (Kris Lane)

groups—now extinct—that inhabited the rugged and hot Minero-Carare River basin, which empties into the "Río Grande," or Magdalena, a few hundred miles northwest of Bogotá. Ad hoc paramilitary expeditions from 1584 to 1587 were of special importance for Vargas Machuca, judging from the frequency of his use of examples and his own service reports and merit petitions. Vargas Machuca claimed mines near the town of La Trinidad de los Muzos (today Muzo), home of the world's finest emeralds, but he appears never to have had the capital to work them. He was, it seems, uninterested in settling down to this or any other moneymaking pursuit. Later "punishments" and "pacifications" took Vargas Machuca to the southern highlands not far from Quito, where he attempted to found a town named for his birthplace, and far northwest into Antioquia, near modern Medellín.

After his first wife's death, Vargas Machuca went to Philip II's crowded court in Madrid to seek reward for his services in 1595. It was a tiresome and humiliating errand, and in the long and costly interim the veteran *indiano* wrote his manual of counterinsurgency warfare, *The Indian Militia and Description of the Indies*, published in 1599. He also wrote a brief manual of horsemanship, *Exercicios de la gineta* (roughly, *Exercises in Light Cavalry*), published by the same house in 1600. With Philip II dead, Philip III's court at last granted Vargas Machuca a post: castellan of Portobelo, on the north coast of Panama. This was not the plum governorship he had expected, and Vargas Machuca's next half-dozen years in Panama left him bankrupt, bitter, and in broken health. It was here that he first drafted his *Defense of the Western Conquests*.

After another expensive stay in Madrid following his Panama term, Vargas Machuca won a better job as governor of the sun-baked pearling island of Margarita, off the coast of Venezuela. It was no Potosí, but Vargas Machuca made the most of another half-dozen years (1609–16) in the business of maintaining Caribbean defenses. Margarita was by this time mostly inhabited by enslaved Africans and their descendants, but a small number of Spanish and creole householders, plus a few hundred native Americans, mostly of Guayquerí ancestry, also remained. As the pearl beds gave out, locals traded contraband tobacco to foreigners, most of them Dutch and English. This activity had been violently suppressed by Spanish naval forces just prior to Vargas Machuca's arrival.

Letters in Seville's Archive of the Indies suggest that Margarita islanders of all sorts were wary of their new governor, a martinet devoted to pleasing the king of Spain for his own benefit. Vargas Machuca's saving grace was that he was not lazy, and his efforts to improve Margarita's fortunes eventually won allies. As governor, he failed to have his jurisdiction expanded to include the nearby coast and several "Carib-infested" islands, but he did manage to outfit and dispatch a new series of "punishments" of neighboring Caribs. Dutch pirates were less of a menace, as his tenure overlapped with the Twelve Years' Truce (1609–21) between Spain and the Netherlands, but this allowed Vargas Machuca to devote considerable attention— and royal funds—to expanding Margarita's forts and urban infra-structure. He also rewrote his *Defense of the Western Conquests* (a.k.a. *Apologetic Discourses*) in 1612, adding a chapter on Margarita. He apparently sent it off for consideration in 1613, possibly to Lima, since it was dedicated to the viceroy of Peru.

After sailing to Spain in 1617 to seek yet another promotion, Vargas Machuca found himself deeper in debt than before, old and encumbered with dependents, and no luckier at court. While in Madrid in 1618 he appears to have edited two manuscript ver-sions of the *Defense* and sought new permissions to publish. Final approval for publication never came. Vargas Machuca expanded and republished his manual of horsemanship twice and then died of an unknown illness in 1622, just after receiving his last promotion. In late 1621 he had been named governor of Antioquia, a gold-mining district in northwest New Granada that, like Margarita, had fallen on hard times.

Had Vargas Machuca survived to take this last hot-country post, it is likely that he would have set about organizing paramilitary raids against the fierce Chocó peoples of the nearby Pacific low-lands. An almost seamless continuation of the process of pillage and enslavement begun on Hispaniola in 1492, war in the Colombian Chocó raged on into the early eighteenth century. As Las Casas might have predicted, the captives who survived, held in encomienda, were made to mine gold.[17] Those who died were replaced with enslaved Africans. The failure to publish his *Defense* aside, it was

17. Caroline Williams, *Between Resistance and Adaptation: Indigenous Peoples and the Colonisation of the Chocó, 1510–1753* (Liverpool: University of Liverpool Press, 2005).

Vargas Machuca's model of imperial expansion, not Las Casas's, that won the day in the Spanish American backcountry.

Vargas Machuca's Text and This Translation

In his equally "brevísima" *Defense of the Western Conquests*, Bernardo de Vargas Machuca attacks each of Las Casas's regional conquest examples, offering his own, frequently off-point counter-narratives from Hispaniola to Peru. He adds the Caribbean island of Margarita, since he knew it so well, and also Chile, about which he held strong opinions. The structure seems sound enough, but Vargas Machuca gets off to a rough start, admitting in his first chapter that he "tires himself" in trying to counter the many exaggerations of the venerable "bishop of Chiapa." The luckless conquistador's first counterexamples to Las Casas's denunciations of atrocities on Hispaniola do not even come from the Caribbean. Yet he is still worth a listen.

Despite some self-deprecating words about his lack of style and erudition, Vargas Machuca says that he is a worthy opponent of Las Casas for two reasons: (1) his "correct" understanding of just war and (2) his wealth of face-to-face experiences with Amerindians, especially in combat. Vargas Machuca's views on just war were fairly simple. Like Sepúlveda, whose writings he uses as a preface, he believed that America's many native peoples were naturally ferocious and/or inclined to commit crimes against nature (and, less surprisingly, Spanish colonists), and as such deserved subjection, if not outright enslavement. It was right to wage war against them owing to their naturally fierce and rebellious nature. Spanish dominion over the Indies was not debatable, thanks to a papal decree based in part on alleged indigenous violations of natural law.

Indeed, by Vargas Machuca's time, a considerable corpus of grants, decrees, and bulls justified "punishment" for a wide range of indigenous infractions, from sodomy to highway robbery. "Conquest" was not even the proper name for what he and others had been doing, Vargas Machuca defiantly states in his *Defense*: it was "pacification." Yet in using these terms (*castigo* and *pacificación*) to defend himself and his conquistador predecessors against the blasts of Las Casas, Vargas Machuca appears unaware that these very words had been officially adopted by the Spanish crown in response to the friar's efforts in 1573. By the time he got to the Indies in 1578, Vargas Machuca was engaged in a different kind of war than those that had occupied Cortés or Pizarro. This was not "virgin soil" conquest but counterinsurgency.

Battlefield experience was less likely to get lost amid the finer points of history and theory, although it, too, was prone to exaggeration and other distortions. Vargas Machuca was proud to point out that he had fought on many fronts by 1612. He had been all over the Caribbean, Mexico, and Peru by the time he composed his *Defense*, and he had certainly traveled to more places and perhaps also interacted with more varieties of "Indians" than his dead opponent, Las Casas.

One of Vargas Machuca's first lines of attack, one taken by many predecessors, was to challenge the friar's understanding of American geography—and with it, demography. Although he does not cite it, Vargas Machuca had published, as a kind of appendix to his 1599 manual for conquistadors, a fairly detailed description of Western Hemisphere lands, seas, rivers, and ports.[18] Where the friar claimed there were thousands of leagues of coast, Vargas Machuca cut them down to hundreds. Where for Las Casas there had been "beehives" of Indians, Vargas Machuca had seen only trackless mangroves.

When it came to illustrating what he believed was wrong with native Americans themselves, Vargas Machuca drew mostly on personal experience in the New Kingdom of Granada, roughly today's Colombia. He mentions Aztec human sacrifice as one of several abominable practices explained away by Las Casas, but since he had never witnessed it, he instead refers to examples of what he considers extreme and unnatural cruelty among the forest-dwelling peoples of Colombia's Magdalena Valley. Here is where Vargas Machuca offers something radically different from Las Casas's scholarly detractors (such as Sepúlveda), and his often bizarre and decontextualized examples, as much as anything else, justify this annotated translation. They contain nuggets of what might be called "perpetrator ethnography." He is an Indian hunter who unwittingly collects gems of indigenous action and custom.

Violent encounters with bellicose lowland indigenous groups, especially the Carib-speaking Muzos and Carares of the middle

---

18. Distances are listed in the brief "Hydrography of the Coasts and Seas of the Indies," *The Indian Militia,* 285–91.

Magdalena, plus years of mundane interaction with the more pacific highland Muisca of the Savanna of Bogotá, led Vargas Machuca to the conclusion that "Indians" in general were naturally cruel, sexually depraved, cowardly, and avaricious—all the traits Las Casas had ascribed to the conquistadors in the *Brevísima relación*. The Hispaniola historian and fellow castle keeper Fernández de Oviedo (who had also briefly fought Carib-speakers in what is today Colombia) had come to the same conclusion well before Vargas Machuca was born. Both shared the same loathing of Las Casas, and both had the same trouble getting published that seemed to plague all the friar's enemies.

Getting published from the imperial fringes, and as a soldier in the Indian wars, was only part of the problem, according to Vargas Machuca. As if a victim of the "Las Casas curse," the author says he wrote the *Defense of the Western Conquests* not once, but twice. At the urging of fellow soldiers stationed in the Panamanian fortress town of Portobelo, he drafted a manuscript around 1603 and sent it to Lima to be printed. It was stolen (or lost) en route, setting up the possibility that someone else might publish it under another name and take credit. If this happened, no such book has come to light.

The second writing, done on the Caribbean island of Margarita in 1612 (corrected in 1618 in Spain), is what has survived. Despite support from prominent Dominicans and other influential patrons—see the laudatory sonnets and other introductory material below—the *Defense of the Western Conquests* was never published in Vargas Machuca's lifetime, or indeed in the whole colonial period. A less generous Dominican, the chronicler Antonio de Remesal, claimed in 1620 that the *Defense,* a quixotic exercise in "fighting the Cid after his death," was rightly denied publication license by the Council of the Indies.[19]

Only in 1879, amid a wave of nostalgia for Spain's Golden Age, was Vargas Machuca's manuscript recovered and set to print—first by Antonio María Fabié, as an appendix to his *Vida y escritos de fray Bartolomé de las Casas,* and then (in the same year) as part of the massive *Colección de documentos inéditos para la historia de España.*[20] There are two known copies of the 1612 manuscript, one

19. Antonio de Remesal, *Historia general de las Indias Occidentales y particular de la Gobernación de Chiapa y Guatemala* (Mexico City: Porrúa, 1988).

20. Bernardo de Vargas Machuca, "Apologías y discursos de las Conquistas Occidentales," in Antonio María Fabié, ed., *Vida y escritos de fray Bartolomé de las Casas*

(which lacks the sixth defense) in Madrid's Palacio Real and the other in the library of the University of Salamanca. Aside from a few brief references by Las Casas specialists, the *Defense of the Western Conquests* has been all but ignored by scholars.[21]

A rare exception to this rule is Aoki Yasuyuki's 1994 Japanese translation of five of the six defenses, appended to Vargas Machuca's much-better-known *Indian Militia* (minus the "Description of the Indies").[22] Aoki presents Vargas Machuca's work as a useful "soldier's" counterpoint to Las Casas, whose *Very Brief Account* is another translated work in the same series. As for mid-twentieth-century scholars interested in the so-called Spanish struggle for justice, Vargas Machuca was mostly brushed off as one of several "lightweight" Las Casas detractors. Even Ramón Menéndez Pidal, who made the audacious claim in 1963 that Las Casas was mentally unstable, gives short shrift to the *indiano* soldier.[23] The great Las Casas specialist Lewis Hanke's response to Menéndez Pidal is almost as dismissive with regard to Vargas Machuca's work and alleged Dominican support.[24]

The Spanish historian María Luisa Martínez de Salinas, whose doctoral dissertation was a thorough biography of Vargas Machuca, published her own transcription of the Salamanca manuscript in

---

(Madrid: Miguel Ginesta, 1879), 2:409–517, and in *Colección de documentos inéditos para las historia de España,* ed. José Sancho Rayón and Francisco de Zabalburu, 112 vols. (Madrid: Miguel Ginesta, 1849–88), 71:201–309. On Fabié, see Christopher Schmidt-Nowara, *The Conquest of History,* 134–35.

21. For example, Marcel Bataillon, in his *Études sur Bartolomé de las Casas* (Paris: Centre de Recherches de l'Institut d'Études Hispaniques, 1965), cites Vargas Machuca's *Defense* only in relation to the failed colonies of Venezuela and Verapaz, Guatemala (132, 200–201). Where Bataillon does offer something valuable is in linking Vargas Machuca to his *indiano* neighbor in highland New Granada, Juan de Castellanos, author of the massive ca. 1592 poem *Elegías de varones ilustres de Indias* (Bogotá: Selene Impresores, 1997). Vargas Machuca may have derived his (mis)understanding of Las Casas's 1518 Venezuela settlement scheme from Castellanos (285–89).

22. Aoki Yasuyuki, trans., *Michi no senshi to no takakai* (Tokyo: Iwanami Shoten, 1994).

23. Menéndez Pidal, *Bartolomé de Las Casas: Su doble personalidad* (Madrid: Espasa-Calpe, 1963), 359–60. The author treats Vargas Machuca generously, but is mostly interested in the fact that his manuscript was denied publication rights as late as 1618.

24. Lewis Hanke, "The Meaning Today of the Las Casas Treatises Published in 1552," and "More Heat and Some Light on the Spanish Struggle for Justice in the Conquest of America," both in *Selected Writings of Lewis Hanke on the History of Latin America* (Tempe: ASU Center for Latin American Studies, 1979), 100 and 47, respectively.

1993.[25] As noted below, it differs in some respects from the 1879 transcription, and most of her minimal annotations refer to these differences. In her introduction, Martínez de Salinas admits that her subject is "less than rigorous" in his attack on Las Casas, but her preliminary study is composed almost entirely of biographical details and discussion of Vargas Machuca's earlier writings. Martínez de Salinas's main contribution may be her insistence that Vargas Machuca intentionally left the legal defense of Spanish American conquest to Sepúlveda, whose response to Las Casas he placed at the start of both of his *Defense of the Western Conquests* manuscripts.[26]

The Mexican historian Benjamín Flores Hernández has also treated the *Defense of the Western Conquests* in some detail, although he expends almost as much energy defending Vargas Machuca's reputation as he does critically assessing his work. He seems at pains to defend the *Defense*. In a more recent essay, Flores Hernández suggests that Vargas Machuca's description of Margarita in his last *Defense* is at least useful for Caribbean history.[27] No one else seems to have cared much for what Hanke called "that doughty fighter."

Conclusion

As for Captain Bernardo de Vargas Machuca, it would seem that his testimony against Las Casas would have very little importance. The fact that he was a soldier with twenty years' experience in the Indies did not necessarily endow him with the ideas, knowledge, and experience of a colonist, or even a conquistador. He may have been a good officer of modest rank, and nothing more.
 —Juan Comas, *"Historical Reality and the Detractors of Father Las Casas"*

25. Bernardo de Vargas Machuca, *Apologías y discursos de las conquistas occidentales,* ed. María Luisa Martínez de Salinas (Ávila, Spain: Junta de Castilla y León, 1993; from original Salamanca manuscript, 1618).

26. Ibid., 8, 26.

27. Benjamín Flores Hernández, "Pelear con el Cid después de muerto: Las *Apologías y discursos de las conquistas occidentales* de Bernardo de Vargas Machuca, en controversia con la *Brevísima relación de la destrucción de las Indias* de Fray Bartolomé de las Casas," in *Estudios de Historia Novohispana* 10 (Mexico City: UNAM, 1991): 45–105; and Flores Hernández, "Bernardo de Vargas Machuca y el Caribe," *Revista Mexicana del Caribe* 14 (2002): 81–103.

As the Spanish-born anthropologist and historian Juan Comas pointed out so witheringly in 1950,[28] as an intellectual exercise Vargas Machuca's attempt to refute Las Casas is arguably a failure. This is not to deny the author's authority as an experienced fighter, much less to judge his qualities as a person, but rather to assess his work as a polemicist in his own time and social context. Spain's claim to the Americas and to the persons and belongings of its native inhabitants was not easily justified by anyone, least of all a late-arriving militiaman who applied *a posteriori* reasoning to vague and tenuous lines of argument, had trouble staying on point, and blithely offered contradictory examples. It would take Lima-born jurist Juan de Solórzano Pereira decades to compose a convincing legal defense of Spanish colonialism, the monumental 1629 *De Indianum jure*, and even it proved a hard sell among Las Casas sympathizers.[29]

Vargas Machuca's *Defense of the Western Conquests* is perhaps best appreciated as a heartfelt and "experientially" informed *Indiano* counterpoint from the margins. Unlike the set of arguments put forth by Sepúlveda, it is not at root a legalistic exercise. This fact, rather than alleged censorship by "Lascasian" partisans, is arguably why it has been ignored. Las Casas's *Brevísima relación* was a polemical tract meant to convince a complacent monarch and his gold-starved subjects to halt their slaughter, however unwitting, of millions of innocent people on the other side of the ocean. As an emotional homily, or sermon, it was not meant to be "objectively" factual, just morally persuasive.

The fact that Spain's enemies seized on Las Casas's exaggerated depictions of conquistador violence and indigenous passivity was not relevant to the *Brevísima relación*'s purpose, and these depictions hardly reflect Las Casas as a thinker. As his extensive historical writings indicate, Las Casas knew very well how to handle contradictory evidence and proved more than capable of narrating a host of colonial ambiguities without resorting to histrionics and snap judgments. To

28. See Juan Comas, "Historical Reality and the Detractors of Father Las Casas," in Friede and Keen, *Bartolomé de las Casas in History*, 514. The essay was first written in 1950 as a rejoinder to José Pérez de Barradas's Fascist-flavored *Los mestizos en América* (Madrid: Cultura Clásica y Moderna, 1948), which used Vargas Machuca to attack Las Casas (135–36).

29. See James Muldoon, *The Americas in the Spanish World Order: The Justification for Conquest in the Seventeenth Century* (Philadelphia: University of Pennsylvania Press, 1994).

Columbus, nowadays routinely demonized, Las Casas was surprisingly sympathetic in his *History of the Indies;* in the *Brevísima relación,* aimed at a different audience, he was all passion. In this "pulpit" version of the story, Cortés, even if he could not be named, was a heartless killer.

Vargas Machuca was at least as passionate, energetic, and driven to be heard as Las Casas when he wrote his *Defense of the Western Conquests.* Seething with anger and feeling abandoned at the colonial fringe, he saw the friar's still-circulating tract as an affront to his honor, his faith, and his patriotism. As the failed conquistador saw it, he and many others of his paramilitary class had served well and valiantly in the name of God and king, only to find a preacher's printed (and illustrated!) insults held up as reward. A rebuttal, even if late, was worth the effort. In this regard Vargas Machuca resembles the "forgotten" conquistador Bernal Díaz del Castillo, but instead of a "True History" of a particular conquest campaign, Vargas Machuca opts for a point-by-point defense of conquest in general.

Vargas Machuca had a lot to say here and in other writings, which were always peppered with incidental ethnographic testimony regarding virtually unknown indigenous cultures. Even historians of colonial Colombia have largely failed to mine his work in this regard, although at least one attempted to defend him in the more conquistador-friendly 1950s. Yet in setting out to defend the conquistadors, among whom he rather lamely counted himself, Vargas Machuca resorted to a rhetorically unconvincing grab bag of geographical corrections and wild generalizations about a single, core Amerindian character even as he offered examples of considerable diversity. "Indians" were universally bad, he ends up having to say, only because Las Casas had said they were universally good.

What Vargas Machuca failed to realize, among other things, was that readers in Europe were more likely to favor Las Casas's generalizations over his own, precisely because they fit with persistent medieval notions of "sinless" antipodal freaks and limitless, verdant, milk-and-honey landscapes across the sea. By taking the negative approach to the "truth" about Indians, and then failing to reconcile contradictory examples he himself offers—such as the "noble" Tlaxcalans of Mexico and "gentle" Guayquerí of Margarita—Vargas Machuca's claim that conquistadors fought just wars and administered just punishments because they were dealing with an inherently evil people falls apart. He had picked a fight with a dead man, and lost.

A Note on the Translation

TIMOTHY F. JOHNSON

For the present translation, we have taken advantage of the two existing manuscripts, initially working from the 1879 version in volume 71 of the *Colección de documentos inéditos para la historia de España* (hereafter *C.D.I.*) edited by José Sancho Rayón and Francisco de Zabalburu. This transcription, as well as those edited by Fabié and Juan Guixé,[1] is from manuscript #2964, stored in the Royal Palace in Madrid. Access to the other manuscript, #2010, housed in the library of the University of Salamanca, provided the definitive source for our translation. This manuscript was virtually ignored until 1993, possibly because, as Lewis Hanke states, quoting Roland Hussey, it was thought to have "no additional information on Las Casas."[2] It does, however, contain more information on its author, Vargas Machuca, as well as his "intention," by including several documents not found in the Royal Palace manuscript. As Benjamín Flores Hernández mentions[3] and María Luisa Martínez de Salinas Alonso points out in the introduction and preliminary study to her 1993 transcription of this second, previously unpublished manuscript, it is the more complete

---

1. This "point-counterpoint" edition with an introduction by Juan Guixé, dated "1913 (?)" by Hanke and Giménez Fernández (1954), contains Las Casas's *Brevísima relación*, followed by Vargas Machuca's defense, "so that the contrast [between the two] may be better seen, and the arguments of each may be weighed" (9). In this later edition, Guixé modernizes the orthography copied faithfully in the previous transcription. See Lewis Hanke and Manuel Giménez Fernández, *Bartolomé de las Casas, 1474–1566: Bibliografía crítica y cuerpo de materiales para el estudio de su vida, escritos, actuación y polémicas que suscitaron durante cuatro siglos* (Santiago de Chile: Fondo Histórico y Bibliográfico José Toribio Medina, 1954)
2. Hanke and Giménez Fernández, *Bartolomé de las Casas*, 211.
3. Flores Hernández, "Pelear con el Cid después de muerto," 52.

of the two, containing a sixth defense—in this case, of Vargas Machuca's own isle of Margarita—along with the epistle by Manso de Contreras,[4] a small glossary of distinctly American terms used by the author, and a deposition defending the Portuguese governor Juan López de Sequeira's conquests in Panama (omitted below due to its length). The Salamanca manuscript appeared ready for publication not only to Hanke, but also to Manuel Villegas Peralta, whose permission to print was signed in 1618 and is included only with this version of the *Defense*.[5]

In her scholarly Spanish edition of the *Defense*, Martínez de Salinas Alonso points out citations, notes, and phrases that were either added or scratched out by Vargas Machuca or his copy editor in the Royal Palace manuscript in order to demonstrate "a scholarship on the part of the author that is not seen in the present [Salamanca] edition . . . [and] for a better analysis of the work, its author, and its content."[6] One gathers that MS #2964 was a working copy, and the Salamanca manuscript, a final draft, should have been published in the first place. We have compared our translation, based upon the original Salamanca manuscript, to both the earlier transcription from 1879 as well as Martínez de Salinas Alonso's definitive annotated edition of 1993. In our edition, we incorporate Vargas Machuca's scholarly references and marginal notes within the body of the text, in parentheses, and note any significant differences between the two manuscripts.

Curiously included in both manuscripts, yet omitted in earlier transcriptions, are the "Twelve Objections" of Ginés de Sepúlveda to Las Casas's arguments before the Royal Council, summarized by Friar Domingo de Soto in 1552. These objections are included in Las Casas's Third Treatise, otherwise known as *Aquí se contiene una disputa o controversia* ("Herein is a dispute or controversy").[7]

---

4. Licenciate Francisco Manso de Contreras, audiencia judge at Santo Domingo, is not to be confused with the Dominican friar Francisco Manso de Contreras, who seems to have been born on Margarita Island and whose sonnet appears directly before the epistle.

5. For further reading on the publication history of the two existing manuscripts, see Flores Hernández, "Pelear con el Cid después de muerto," 45–105.

6. Vargas Machuca, *Apologías y discursos*, 28 (my translation).

7. Found in Las Casas's *Tratados* (286–329). In his introduction, Lewis Hanke makes reference to Vargas Machuca's "indignant" elaboration of his "tedious and impassioned reply" to a French translation of the *Brevísima relación* (xv). He notes that Vargas Machuca based his arguments on the doctrine of Sepúlveda, and that he

Vargas Machuca's inclusion of this fragment serves as a direct link between him and Sepúlveda, imaginary brothers in arms against Las Casas. Omitted in all but the most recent transcription, the text of Sepúlveda's Objections was a rare publication of the time, and Flores Hernández suggests it was included to secure its existence and future, as well as to provide an erudite and historical buttress to Vargas Machuca's argument.[8]

After hacking our way into the uncharted territory of our previous translation of Vargas Machuca's *Indian Militia*, his matter-of-fact, military voice guiding us into combat became familiar. In his *Defense*, however, his voice has acquired an impatient and (yes, Professor Hanke) *impassioned* strain. Here we see the author both as legal duelist and storyteller, presenting his case with anecdotes from the rainforest, and hammering home his points with still more laudatory references to Cortés or deprecatory insinuations toward the unpatriotic, misguided, and misleading "Bishop of Chiapa." In this translation, we have sought to preserve the antiquated feel of Vargas Machuca's voice by making use of Latin cognates where possible and practical. We have, at times, allowed him to ramble on with page-long sentences in a style typical of the age, but have made adjustments for clarification with punctuation and English syntax. As in *The Indian Militia*, spelling of place names has been standardized, and brackets and italics have been minimized.

---

judiciously includes laudatory sonnets written by a few of Las Casas's Dominican brethren as if to demonstrate that not every clergyman was against the conquest. The "French translation" in question is most likely the copper-engraved 1598 or 1599 De Bry edition. See also Adorno, *Polemics of Possession*, 338–9, footnote 38.

8. Flores Hernández, "Pelear con el Cid después de muerto," 67–68.

The cause for which the Christians have slain and destroyed so many and such infinite numbers of souls has been simply to get, as their ultimate end, the Indians' gold of them, and to stuff themselves with riches in a very few days, and to raise themselves to high estates—without proportion to their birth or breeding, it should be noted—owing to the insatiable greed and ambition that they have had, which has been greater than any the world has ever seen before.

—Fray Bartolomé de las Casas

DEFENSE AND DISCOURSE

OF THE

WESTERN CONQUESTS

BY

DON BERNARDO DE VARGAS MACHUCA

GOVERNOR AND CAPTAIN GENERAL OF THE ISLE OF MARGARITA

AGAINST THE TREATISE

DESTRUCTION OF THE INDIES

WRITTEN BY

DON FRAY BARTOLOMÉ DE LAS CASAS,

BISHOP OF CHIAPA IN THE YEAR 1552

DIRECTED TO HIS MOST EXCELLENT LORD DON JUAN DE MENDOZA
Y LUNA, MARQUIS OF MONTES CLAROS AND MARQUIS OF CASTIL
DE VAYUELA, LORD OF THE VILLAS OF LA HIGUERA DE LAS DUEÑAS,
EL COLMENAR, EL CARDOSO, EL VADO Y VALCONETE, LIEUTENANT
VICEROY OF THE KING OUR LORD, HIS GOVERNOR AND CAPTAIN
GENERAL OF THE KINGDOMS AND PROVINCES OF PERU, TIERRA
FIRME AND CHILE, ETC.

Translated from the Spanish by Timothy F. Johnson

Presentation

We understand, though their virtue be hidden, the workings of the lodestone, whose attributes, upon comparison, are found in every prince in just proportion; for if it is well considered, they both captivate and carry one's will along with them. And if they do not manifest themselves every time it is because there is no need, and though it is true I do not possess them, I have not wished to waste time invoking the many virtues with which Your Excellency was naturally gifted, perfected with such great prudence proclaimed by fame; and, as Aristotle says, men must cling to virtue as to a sacred place from which they may not be excluded; and by itself, the idea of virtue pleases and attracts. This lodestone has led me far from shore to seek out Your Excellency and offer the labor of this treatise entitled *Defense of the Western Conquests,* and I am certain that, being seen favorably, the courage to sail throughout the rest of the world will grow, being its primary intention, following that which don Fray Bartolomé de las Casas, or Cassaos, Bishop of Chiapa, wrote in the year 1552. And though I am certain it will cause many disputes, within Spain as well as without, and that the Bishop will find innumerable defenders and seconds incited by the enmity they have for our nation, and that those at home will look upon the arguments of a religious and learned bishop more favorably than upon those of a conquering soldier, all things considered, in its defense, following that of Your Excellency, I submit, as a second, its own true justification; and upon those words of Pliny that say how in great things reason must be more powerful than authority, and those of Cicero that say how that which is true must be worth more than opinion, and of Plutarch, that the function of reason is to make all things agreeable, I beg Your Excellency to receive this under your protection and refuge, as I hope to God the arguments upon which it is based may be agreeable to you, and likewise that each man should comprehend it. And so I state, being favorably seen, that no refuge better suited to its purpose could be found, nor is there anything Your Excellency must defend more, as one who has and presently possesses all the governance of the Indies with such great experience and knowledge and with supreme command over all of them. May God keep Your Excellency, this your servant desires.

From Margarita, August 10 of the year 1612.
Don Bernardo de Vargas y Machuca

To the Reader

Self-defense being, such as it is, a natural thing, I have not been able
to avoid defending my own honor and that common to our nation,
that with pious countenance and appearances the learned Bishop of
Chiapa, don Fray Bartolomé de las Casas, or Cassaos, attempted to
tarnish in the discourse he wrote in the year 1552 with that con-
temptible title *The Destruction of the Indies,* in which he attempted
to depict as cruelties the legal punishments in all the Western Indies
that the conquerors executed (and presently carry out) upon the
Indians for heinous crimes that were (and are) committed every day.
And [his treatise] has had such an effect on the Huguenots, conform-
ing to their ancient malice and scorning the great Christianity of
Spain, that they have published tracts that describe the Indies with
various forms of cruelties, citing the Bishop of Chiapa with chapters
from his treatise, some that he truly wrote and some they invented,[1]
based upon these words written against good opinion, clemency, and
Christian piety; and though it is true that the primary cause of such
a motive was given by the Bishop by having written so clearly and
given such a cruel name to legal punishments, nevertheless it is not
correct that they should be understood thusly, but rather they are
owed remuneration as pacifications, permitted and just. And if the
Bishop, according to the ill-intentioned information he had, affirmed
them as truths, with how much more reason may I, with my own
experience, defend them? It is unjust to damage everything along
with the particular sins of one conqueror that the Bishop should find
soulless, placing in such a condition the worthy names that so many
illustrious men, at the cost of their own blood and with such dangerous labors, so arduously gained and defended. When truth and justice
are not found within such a great body of evidence, the reasons found
in careful conjectures will easily demonstrate that if one considers
that the primary intention of the conquerors in their settlements was
none other than to bring souls to heaven and vassals to their king,

1. For the best study of the lavishly illustrated publications of Theodor de Bry
and sons, which Vargas Machuca probably had in mind, see Michiel van Groesen, *The
Representations of the Overseas World in the De Bry Collection of Voyages (1590–
1634)* (Leiden: Brill, 2008). Interestingly, Groesen finds that the De Brys chose not to
include Las Casas's *Brevísima relación* in their famous *America* collection, possibly to
avoid Catholic censorship, although they did publish illustrated translations of it sepa-
rately in 1598 and 1599.

as well as their own honor and duty, then cruelly destroying the Indians, as the Bishop says, would end everything without gathering souls for heaven nor vassals for the King nor any advantage whatsoever, their cruel appetite feeding only upon tyrannies. It is this that has obligated me, as an interested party, to make a similar discourse in defense of the deed of the conquests and the reputation of the Spanish nation, as one who has had much experience with them; though in order to do so with satisfaction and duty, I find myself lacking elegance and with the fear of bringing this defense to light, being as it is such a difficult matter and of such importance; persuaded, however, by worthy people to take it into my charge, I swore myself to it. If I should manage to satisfy, may it be attributed to Divine Providence, considering that I am a soldier and follow good intentions and Christian duty, that in this case it will be sufficient to consider my reason, for with it, no creature will judge it as anything less; and as the wise say, [reason] is served by law, and it is the soul of law. And because the Doctor [Juan] Ginés de Sepúlveda, chronicler of Emperor Charles V, sustained royal law against the aforementioned Bishop, and did not write of the deeds of the conquests since he lacked [firsthand knowledge of] them, and because it is my responsibility for the reasons already referred to, I have, in order to better present the defense, presented the existing [i.e., Sepúlveda's twelve] objections first, as the laws [should be understood] so that the deeds may be justified, not disputing the basic principles upon which they are founded, but rather supposing them to be true and fair and justly established by the kings of Spain, as shown in the bulls of His Holiness [the pope], demonstrating only the manner in which the Spaniards carried them out and that they were not tyrannies. To such an end I leave the *quod quid est* of the justice and cause of the war, and pursue the deed and reason, asking the discriminating reader to receive this treatise in his good graces.

Be aware that if [the reader] should happen upon another [treatise] addressing this topic, in verse or in prose, printed in Spain or abroad some years ago, it is my work and reasoning, for fifteen years ago, while I governed Portobelo, this same book was stolen, having been sent for printing to the city of Lima, in Peru. It seemed right to make this warning having had several leads in the case, so that the reader who should come upon this defense by two authors will know its true owner, though the same work may manifest the truth, as it cannot remain hidden for long. [Madrid, 1618]

From Friar Pedro de Umana, of the Order of Preachers

Sonnet

Bernardo in valor, in science, Apollo,
Elegant Cicero, shrewd Scotus,
Spanish Euclid, learned Seneca,
New Plato, in our world alone.

Thy fame, that from pole to pole
Declares thy virtue to the outmost,
Brought me to thee to make good my pledge
Upon the shoulders of furious Aeolus.

The vow was to be eternally thine,
And now that I have beheld thee
And the fruit of thy peregrine wit,

I vow to announce to generations
Thy nobility, valor, and perfect being,
With which thou aspire to the divine.

From Friar Adrian de Padilla, of the Order of Preachers

Sonnet

He wears his arms and wields his sword
In the time of venturous Alfonso,
Bernardo the offended and valorous,
Defends his harried Spain.

And thou, Bernardo, in thy bold hand
In the time of miraculous Philip,
Take up the quill to win and return
Ruined Spaniards' honor.

Perhaps thou wilt share fame with [St.] Bernardo,
For the sword and the pen are equals
Both offer rewards of crown and glory.

And tho' I praise thee late, I am not belated
In knowing Bernardos immortal
And dedicate my art to their memory.

From Friar Raimundo de Cárdenas, of the Order of Preachers

Sonnet

Eminent virtue, prudence and art
Illustrious Bernardo, the glory of this earth,
Heaven gave to thee as to none other,
Nor in all the world what it shares with thee.[2]

For in actions of bloody Mars
Thy lineage flew highest,
And with thy Christian and holy zeal
The orb from end to end is filled.

Fame reveals itself by proclaiming thee,
Likening thee, in greatness and acumen,
To the majesty of this our age.

From pole to pole flieth thy name,
In knowledge, thou wilt gain the heights supreme
As can be seen in this thy book.

2. The Royal Palace transcription reads, "The qualities it shares with thee alone" (*CDI*, 209).

From Friar Francisco Manso de Contreras, of the Order of Preachers

Sonnet

So from the peaceful Ganges to the Nile,
And from swift Tanais[3] to the Ebro,
With adornments of thread and juniper,
On plates of gold and panes of beryl,

Fame inscribes with the greatest art
What, in my ignorance, I shatter attempting,
When in my verses I celebrate thy valor,
Famous Bernardo, affront to Camillus.

I beg thee, moved by thy valor
Tho' the word of a king be it not,
To fulfill what is just, for thy merits abound,

And thou shalt give unto fame what is hers.
May light shine upon thy book eternal
In future and former times.

---

3. That is, the river Don.

Epistle by Licentiate Francisco Manso de Contreras,
Judge in the Royal Audiencia of Panama, to don Bernardo de Vargas
Machuca, Governor and Field Marshal of the Isle of Margarita.

If men did not grow fond of the sweetness of the fruits of their labors, there would be few who would undertake their enterprises. That of this book [i.e., the enterprise or purpose] is so important that it should be held in high esteem, not only for having such a glorious end, but especially because of its good intention; for it is sufficient to strive and wish for great things, and none can do better than defend the honor and reputation of those who won this New World, the justified manner of its discovery, and the conversion of its natives to our Holy Catholic faith, that though it is the most heroic deed done by any nation, and more to the service of God and the flourishing of the Royal Crown of Spain, there have been the Bishop of Chiapas and others who, with no experience or foundation, procured to slander her; [but] now there will not be enough [of them], having such a great defender such as Your Honor and the defenses of your book, where, with great propriety, you address, honor, and justify the matter of these conquests, and I know of none other who speaks and acts in these discoveries like Your Honor, nor to whom we who have served His Majesty and His Royal Ancestors owe so much, for Your Honor knew better than any other how to give our labors and services the value they deserve; and I have involved myself in this account because in the eight years that I governed the provinces of Santa Marta and Río de la Hacha [on the Caribbean coast of present-day Colombia], I settled several towns and rebuilt others, [and] I reduced and brought to peace all the rebelling Indians who killed friars and clerics and many Spaniards with severity and cruelties never seen before. Up to now, little has been done regarding these services, for [their accounts] arrive cold in the eyes of those who would reward them, [as if they were] water under the bridge. And I believe without a doubt that from now on, this book will be the great solicitor of the reward owed to each one, and when Your Honor has no other [reward] but the obligation we have in serving you and thanking you for the work and care you have brought to our defense, the time spent will not have been in vain. I assure Your Honor that this book will no doubt be particularly well-received by His Majesty and by the lords of his Council, for in order to govern these kingdoms well there should be a certain and true record of the manner of their pacification, and of the necessity of punishing the Indians who rebel with little or no cause, and of the explanations of the common libel unjustly imposed upon the conquerors. These and other things to this purpose will be found in this book, and may it be printed quickly so that others may enjoy its fruit and the work of Your Honor be accomplished; may Our Lord guard you with the greatness you deserve. Isle of Margarita, October 25 of the year 1609.

Manso de Contreras, Licentiate

[Vargas Machuca here inserts Juan Ginés de Sepúlveda's twelve-point response to Bartolomé de las Casas.]

THE CONTROVERSY BETWEEN THE BISHOP OF CHIAPAS AND DOCTOR SEPÚLVEDA IN THE YEAR 1552, IN WHICH THE BISHOP CONDEMNED THE RIGHT OF THE WESTERN CONQUESTS AND THE DOCTOR DEFENDED IT WITH ELEGANCE.

After seeing the summary that the Very Reverend Father Maestro Friar Domingo de Soto was assigned to make of the Assembly, as has been stated, Doctor Sepúlveda brought forth from it twelve objections, responding to each. They are the following.[4]

PROLOGUE OF DOCTOR SEPÚLVEDA TO THE MEMBERS OF THE ASSEMBLY

Illustrious and magnificent lords: now your lordships and graces, as judges, have listened to the Lord Bishop of Chiapas for five or six days while he read the book with which for many years he has been occupied [i.e., the *Apologetic History*], and [in which] he has gathered all the reasons invented by himself and by others in order to prove the conquest of the Indies unjust, first subjecting the barbarians and then preaching the Gospel to them, which is the approach our kings and nation have reasonably taken up to now, in accordance with the [papal] bull and consent of Pope Alexander VI. I therefore beg that, as I defend the justification and authority of the Apostolic See and the justice and honor of our kings and nation, you listen to me with attentive souls while I briefly and frankly respond to his objections and arguments, for I hope to clearly demonstrate, with the help of God and the truth I defend, that everything brought in opposition [to conquest] is with frivolous reasons and of little weight to such dignified and learned judges, whom one cannot suspect would place any other reservation between the justice and truth that matter so much. I come to the point, then, with brief words, for with persons so occupied in great things and in the governing of the republic, long-windedness would be discourteous.

4. Although included in the original manuscripts, this translation of the Twelve Objections of Juan Ginés de Sepúlveda is based on the transcription by Juan Pérez de Tudela Bueso, with translations of Latin portions (in italics) by Agustín Millares Carlo and Rafael Moreno in Fray Bartolomé de las Casas, *Tratados* (Mexico City: Fondo de Cultura Económica, 1965), 1:287–329; Latin translations from 2:1299–1303. Translations of biblical verses are from the King James Version.

FIRST OBJECTION

[Fray Bartolomé de las Casas] first claims that many other nations beyond the Promised Land were idolatrous, [but] were not destroyed by the people of Israel; and that those within the Promised Land were not destroyed for idolatry and therefore it is not a just cause for war.[5]

To this I respond that for the same reason one could infer that highway robbery is not a crime worthy of death because many robbers have not been given such a punishment. I say, therefore, that the inhabitants of the Promised Land were destroyed for idolatries as well as for human sacrifice, as the Holy Scriptures say in Deuteronomy, chapters 9 and 12, and Leviticus, 18 and 20. Other peoples (whose impieties were not so apparent) could be subjected to the faithful nation of the Jews by war because of their faithlessness and idolatry, as the words in Deuteronomy 20:15 declare: *Thus shalt thou do unto all the cities which are very far off from thee, which are not of the cities of these nations*, as the interlinear gloss states. These words come after having described the manner one must have in making war upon them. And with regard to what the Lord Bishop claims, that the reason for destroying the peoples of the Promised Land was not to fulfill the promise God made to Abraham, I say that when God promised it to him, he explained why (Genesis 15). It was not given to him to replace those [lands] they already had, saying that even at that time the evils of the Amorites [i.e., idolatrous Canaanites later defeated by Joshua] had not happened. And to his claim that the words cited from Deuteronomy 20 mean that when the Jews should make war for other just reasons, but not for unfaithfulness or idolatry, I say that this is against the interlinear gloss, for as there were other just causes for war, it could be justifiably made, even if they were of one religion. And to his claim that the examples in the Old Testament do not have to be imitated, I respond that so it is in some things, but not in the precepts and natural laws, which

5. Sepúlveda turns Las Casas's reading of the Old Testament around, using the example of the Israelites in the time of Joshua and other warrior-iconoclasts as evidence of divine approval of spreading the Gospel by war. Sepúlveda quickly appeals to classical thought by arguing that idolatry, or direct worship of material objects, is a practice contrary to natural law (mostly as elaborated by Aristotle). As this claim is difficult to sustain without reverting to biblical authority or at least to Thomas Aquinas's interpretation of the Ten Commandments as divine "clarifications" of natural law, Sepúlveda conflates idolatry with human sacrifice, which he returns to in the eleventh objection. On early Spanish debates over natural law with regard to native American peoples, see, for example, Pagden, *Fall of Natural Man*, 48–50.

must always and in every case be followed by all people, faithful
or not, such as [those regarding] idolatry, that was most severely
punished among various [peoples]. St. Cyprian writes these words
about the precepts and grave punishments: *Because, if these precepts*
regarding the cult of God and the rejection of idols were kept before
the coming of Christ, even more should they be kept after His com-
ing. These words are cited in question 23, chapter 5 of *Si audieris.*
What is more, we are not saying that war must be brought upon
these idolatrous Indians in order to kill them and destroy them like
those in the Promised Land, but rather in order to subject them and
end their idolatry and evil practices, and to remove the impediments
to the preaching of the Gospel.

SECOND OBJECTION

To his claim that the words from the Gospel of Luke 14:23: *Compel*
them to come in, do not refer to armed physical violence but rather
spiritual [persuasion] by exhortations and miracles, and because
there are some who interpret them in this way, I respond that the
same words in the Holy Scriptures allow various interpretations, as
the sacred Doctors testify; but this [interpretation] that the words
refer to physical coercion is not mine, but of St. Augustine in Epistles
48 and 50 and the last, *Vincentium, Bonifacium, Donatum,* citation
23, question 4, and of St. Gregory, Epistle 23 from the first book
and [Epistle] 60 from the ninth [book], and of the entire Church
that held this interpretation not only in word, but even in acts, as
St. Augustine declares in the cited epistles, saying that the power
of the emperors over heretics and pagans came from the Church,
and citing in the last epistle these words from the Psalm [138:4]:
All the kings of the earth shall praise thee, adding, *The more this is*
accomplished, the more authority the Church has, such that it not
only invites but compels them to good. This power [is thus] founded
upon these words from the Gospel: *Compel them to come in.* And in
Epistle 50, he condemns the opinion of those who say these words
must not refer to physical coercion but rather spiritual and miraculous [coercion].

THIRD OBJECTION

To his claim that physical coercion is only to be used against heretics who have received the faith and not against pagans, and that
St. Augustine speaks only of heretics in the places he cites, I respond

that it is true that in those three epistles he argues against heretics, but in this same dispute he adds the cause for the pagans in many places, primarily in Epistle 48, page 110.[6] And even in such a manner, that by the just and greater power the Church had over the Gentiles, ending their idolatry and pagan rituals (the justness of which no Christian doubted, as he himself states), this proves that war against heretics is just, *Ut habetur,* 23, q. 4, chap. *Non invenitur,* where he says, *Who among us (that is, we Catholics), who among you (that is, you heretics), do not praise the laws given by the emperors against the pagan sacrifices?* and so on. And if those who hold this opinion say this power made the Gentiles subjects of the Emperor, that does not preclude it from being physical force, which, if it were unjust, should be applied less to subjects than to foreigners. How much more was it also used against those who were not subjects in the time of St. Gregory, because of the wars Gennadius made upon the Gentiles, because only after they were made subjects could they easily preach the Gospel to them, as in chapter *Si non,* 23, q. 4, of which we will speak later.[7] And how must this physical coercion be carried out in order to preach to the unfaithful and to end their idolatry even if it is against their will, and thus convert them? Gentle and loving persuasion must be used so they convert willingly, and in this way no force is necessary. And this is what the chapter *De iudeis* says; and the chapter *Qui sincera dis,* 45; and that of St. Thomas and St. Augustine: *For none should be forced to faith or to belief.*

FOURTH OBJECTION

To his claim that the saints never urged the Christian kings to make war against the Gentiles in order to end their idolatry, and that one does not read that St. Sylvester urged Constantine to make war against the pagans for this reason, I respond that neither did I say that St. Sylvester urged Constantine to make war against the Gentiles, but rather to end their idolatry with law, with the penalty of death and loss of property, to whomever might most practice it, as

---

6.   Here and elsewhere, Sepúlveda seems to refer to page numbers from a Spanish edition of St. Augustine.

7.   Gregory the Great (ca. 540–604 C.E.) praised Gennadius, exarch, or royal governor, of Byzantine North Africa and Andalusia, but the expansion of papal authority was soon cut short by the Arab invasion. See Susan Raven, *Rome in Africa,* 3rd ed. (New York: Routledge, 1993), 221–22.

he did. For thus it is believed that Constantine did not make that law, but rather, because of the persuasion of the Christians, and primarily of the Pope St. Sylvester who converted and baptized him, for it is consistent with the testimony of St. Augustine, mentioned above, that this law was approved by all Christians. But I say urging kings to [make] just wars is the responsibility of prelates and primarily of the Pope, such as [when] Pontiff Adrian urged Charlemagne to declare war on the Lombards; of which St. Thomas writes in 2nd [book], 2nd [epistle], q. 40, art. 1, *ad* 3, giving the reason and saying: *All authority or art or virtue to which the end [i.e., objective] belongs should make use of those things that are for the end. Wars and earthly things, in a faithful people, should lead, as an end, to the divine spiritual good considered by the clerics. And therefore, clerics have [the duty] of using and inducing others to fight just wars.* And for this reason St. Gregory, as it clearly appears in letter 23 of his first book, praises and urges Gennadius, who acted upon the authority of the Emperor in Africa, to make war upon the Gentiles, so that once they had been subjected the Gospel could be preached to them without impediment. For this they first had to end their idolatry, and he highly praised this deed: *It is sufficient to urge in order to accomplish the objective, whoever with great praises gives the order to accomplish it.* Also St. Thomas 2nd, 2nd, q. 10, art. 11, alluding to the actions of Constantine, says: *The religious customs of the unfaithful should not be tolerated by any means. They may have been tolerated by the Church in other times, when the multitude of unfaithful was great, that is, before Christian princes existed who could compel them.* And in article 8, declaring the cause for the wars and the compulsion of the Gospel that Gennadius made upon the Gentiles, these words are written: *The unfaithful, who never received faith, should in no way be forced to faith so that they themselves believe; they may be forced, however, by the faithful (if possible) not to hinder faith with blasphemies or with evil persuasions or, in addition, with declared persecutions.* For the unfaithful who are not subject to Christians hinder faith in many ways, because they do not allow preachers, rather they kill them, and it should be known that they try to turn those who are converted back to their error with evil persuasions or clear persecutions and with blasphemy, because of their idolatry. For, as the same [citation] states in question 94, article 3, *ad* 2: *Idolatry contains great blasphemy and impedes the work of faith.* Following this doctrine,

Nicolas of Lyra, in *Numerorum* chap. 31, states: *One cause for just war is the war against the region that blasphemes against God with idolatries.*[8] This is why St. Thomas, following those words, says, *Those faithful to Christ frequently make wars upon the unfaithful, not to force them to believe, but to force them not to impede faith,* taking that word *frequenter* from the aforementioned epistle of St. Gregory and *compellant* from the Gospel. And regarding what the Lord Bishop says, that Gennadius made war upon his subjects or against his allies, all this is false. For these peoples against whom he made war were not Roman subjects but neighbors of the Roman Empire in the interior part of Africa (as St. Gregory himself declares at the end of the same epistle, saying, *"neighboring* peoples"). And St. Gregory himself declares that war was not made upon them because they were their enemies or for other reasons, but only in order to expand the Christian republic, and so the name of Christ could be preached to them after their subjection. In this way the wars of Gennadius, just as the law of Constantine, would accomplish primarily the correction and salvation of the unfaithful. For to say the law of Constantine was enacted primarily to prevent the idolatrous from upsetting the Christians among them is clearly false. The Catholics were upset more by the heretics and were more damaged by example and words, arguing with them every day while calling themselves Christians; but the law made against them was principally so they would be corrected and saved, as St. Augustine shows in many places in Epistles 48 and 50 and the last, which are *Vincentium, Bonifacium, Donatum,* cited in Decree 23, q. 4. And the same reason was in the law against the pagans, as St. Augustine himself shows in the same epistles, primarily in 48, page 116, where these words are written: *Pagans are less able to blaspheme against the laws the Christian emperors issued against idol-worshipers; nevertheless, many of them repented and were converted to the living and true God, and every day they are converted.*

FIFTH OBJECTION

To his claim that the Pope has no jurisdiction over the unfaithful because of the authority of St. Paul in Corinthians 5:12–13: *For what have I to do to judge them also that are without? . . . But them that*

---

8.   Nicolas of Lyra (1270–1349) was a Franciscan famous for biblical exegesis. See Philip Krey and Lesley Smith, eds., *Nicholas of Lyra: The Senses of Scripture* (Leiden: Brill, 2000).

are without God judgeth. I respond that the meaning of those words is thus: Why must I, in vain, judge the customs of the unfaithful who do not freely obey as Christians nor whom I may correct? For neither I nor the Church have earthly powers to do it, but even if I do not judge them, God will. As St. Augustine says in the epistle *Vincentium,* p. 116, the custom of the Church is to correct those it can and tolerate those it cannot, leaving them to the judgment of God. The same is said in the epistle *Marcellinum,* p. 116: *We must tolerate (he says), if we cannot correct them, those of the republic who would desire existence,* [despite] *unpunished vices, that the first Romans included and increased with virtues.* And it speaks of the Roman Gentiles who said the Roman Empire and Republic was lost because of the Christian religion. Therefore, it is not prudent to place oneself in a situation from which one cannot escape, nor is it the duty of an apostle to require that the unfaithful account for and live as Christian a life as the Christians. However, seeking to convert them and preaching the Gospel to them and obtaining all that is necessary for this with all his strength is, indeed, the duty of an apostle, as declared by the lives of St. Paul and the other apostles, as well as the deaths they suffered because of it. For this is true: the Pope has the power to preach the Gospel as well as the natural laws contained in the Decalogue [i.e., Ten Commandments], himself or through others, to all the unfaithful in the world, as there is a precept [in the book of] Matthew, last chapter [verse 28:16]; [and] Mark 16 [verse 15]. This power, though it primarily relates to spiritual things, is not excluded from earthly things where these lead to the spiritual, as St. Thomas teaches, *De regimine principum,* book 3, chap. 13. Because he himself says, 2nd, 2nd, q. 40, arts. 2 and 3: *The authority to which the end belongs should make use of those things that belong to the end.* This natural decree is explained through the Church in *De officio, de lege,* chapters *Praeterea, Prudentia,* and *Suspicionis,* where he says whoever is given the responsibility for the principal enterprise is also understood to be responsible for all accessory things that facilitate the purpose, as well as those things without which the enterprise cannot be done. And not being able to do something is understood to mean that which cannot be done because of many difficulties: this is an impossibility, according to Aristotle, *Metaphysics* 5. And in any enterprise, the objective is principal [i.e., primary], and the things that make it possible are called accessories.

SIXTH OBJECTION

To his claim that Christ did not give St. Peter power over all the world because he did not have it *en actu* but rather only *en potencia*,[9] to this I say the power given to Christ, mentioned in the last chapter of Matthew,[10] was the right to shelter and rule and govern his sheep in the entire land where he was called shepherd (John 10), as it is customary in the Holy Scripture to call princes and kings shepherds. He gave this right to his vicar (John 21:16) with these words: *Peter, feed my sheep.* For the lambs of the Lord are not only Christians, but the unbelieving as well, as Christ himself declares (John 10:14), saying, *I am the good shepherd, and know my sheep, and am known of mine.* It is clear that he means the faithful; and later he says [verse 16]: *And other sheep I have, which are not of this fold; them also I must bring,* understood to be the unfaithful, as the scholars declare. And in order to gather these sheep He sent the apostles throughout all the world saying, *Go ye into all the world, and preach the gospel to every creature* (Mark 16:15). Therefore Christ and his vicar had jurisdiction over all the world, as the second Psalm [verse 8] also shows: *Ask of me, and I shall give thee the heathen for thine inheritance, and the uttermost parts of the earth for thy possession.* And to say that Christ has this power and right potentially and not in actuality is to contradict the Gospel, because of this premise: [If] *they do not have in actuality, then they do not have; it is not actuality, therefore it simply is not,* as Aristotle teaches in the ninth book of *Metaphysics.* And if it says potential: *By custom: whoever truly has the custom also has actuality, for custom is a certain act* (Aristotle, *De anima* 2, in 12, q. 49, 1); just as the King of Spain, when he sleeps or plays, has the right *en habitu* of ruling Spain, and he is king truly and *en actu,* even though he is not wielding power over the empire at that moment. And as St. Paul says, in Hebrews 2:8: *For in that he put all in subjection under him, he left nothing that is not put under him.* He speaks of subjection *per fidem,* which is in all the faithful, but this does not exclude the universal [subjection] of all the world in order to keep the law of nature and preach the Gospel and do all the other things that lead to this end. Regarding the authority alleged by St. Augustine, *De puero centurionis: It is ours to speak to Christians,*

---

9. "In actuality" and "potentially," Aristotelian terms from *Metaphysics.*
10. Verse 18, "All power is given unto me in heaven and on earth."

what does it interest me to judge those who are outside? I say these
words are to be interpreted just as we interpreted those above in the
answer to the Fifth Objection. And regarding what St. Augustine
says in his sixth sermon, *De puero centurionis,* with respect to the
breaking of idols, all is aimed against the fury of certain heretics
called "circumcellions"[11] who went to the well-known solemn ceremonies of the pagans, where there was a great multitude of people,
in order to break idols so that they would be killed, believing that
by doing this they were serving God and would become martyrs, as
St. Augustine himself refers to in Epistle 50 of *Bonifacium,* criticiz-
ing such madness and saying that it is not the sorrow that makes a
martyr, but the cause. And here he says God did not send them to
break their idols indiscriminately, but rather when we have them in
our power, as Daniel did when he broke the idol given to him by King
Darius (Daniel 14). And he ordered the people of Israel to break the
statues after they had taken possession of the Promised Land, and not
at a time when they could not be broken without an uproar or danger
to the faithful, as it was in the times of St. Augustine, when there
were many powerful idol-worshipers among the Christians, and if
they wished to break the idols, they would have resisted and there
would have been a great conflict between Christians and Gentiles. For
though the Emperor was Christian, he did not wish to treat the Gentiles as severely as Constantine had. After this, Julian the Apostate
[Roman emperor 361–63 C.E.] persecuted the Christians, and because
of the great resistance the Gentiles made against that law of Constantine, other emperors tolerated the rites of the Gentiles in order
to avoid unrest in the Empire, as seen in what St. Ambrose wrote in
Epistles 30 and 31, that the Gentiles at that time were powerful, that
there were not only many in the Roman Senate, but even the prefect
of the city, Symmachus [Quintus Aurelius Symmachus, ca. 340–402
C.E.], was a Gentile. And this is what St. Thomas says in 2nd, 2nd, art.
11: *The religious customs of the unfaithful should not be tolerated
by any means, unless it is to avoid some evil, that is, to avoid turmoil
or the fall that could come of this, or the impediment of those who,
thus tolerated, little by little are converted to the faith. For such a
cause, the Church also tolerated the religious customs of the heretics
and pagans in other times, when the multitude of the unfaithful*

11. Literally "rovers among the peasants," a semilegendary sect of early North Afri-
can Christians known for violently seeking out martyrdom.

was great. Therefore, St. Augustine, who was younger in the time of St. Ambrose, says that the Christians did not break the idols of the Gentiles because they did not have the power or the ability to do so without agitation and danger, nor were they obligated by divine law to do so if they could not do so without such difficulties, as it would be when the Christians were so many and so powerful they could do it safely and without danger, or when the Gentiles returned to the Christians, for then they themselves would help to break them. And the illustrious authority of St. Augustine must be understood in this way, for the power to end the idolatry of the Gentiles in spite of them, under penalty of death and loss of property, as Constantine did, is licit and holy. St. Augustine himself affirms this with the approval of all Christians (question 23, chapter 4, *Non invenitur;* and St. Thomas, where cited; and St. Gregory in Epistle 6 of book 9), greatly praising Constantine for such a deed.

SEVENTH OBJECTION

Regarding his claim that the canon lawyers, referring to the chapter *quod super hijs, de voto,* when they say that the Church may make war and punish idol-worshipers and those who do not follow the law of nature, one must consider whether the lands are occupied by Christians or they blaspheme the Creator and impede faith, or coinciding with other just causes, I say that this is clearly a conspiracy. For those scholars say that for this cause alone, of not keeping the law of nature or being idol-worshipers, they can be conquered and punished. For it would be folly to say they can be conquered for only blasphemy, and not for idolatry, which is the gravest of sins and includes within it infidelity and blasphemy, as we said above, according to the authority of St. Thomas, as faith refutes the deed (2nd, 2nd, q. 94, art. 3, *ad secundum*).

EIGHTH OBJECTION

Regarding his claim that these Indians are not barbarians to be forced to obey the prudent and the humane, since one may not call barbarians those who have cities and order [*policía*], I say barbarians (as St. Thomas says in *Politicorum I,* first lesson) are understood to be those who do not live according to natural reasoning and have evil customs publicly accepted by all; this may be because of a lack of religion, where men live as brutes, or because of evil customs and the lack of good doctrine and punishment. That these men are of little capacity and with perverse customs is proved by what is said by almost all who return from there [i.e., the western Indies], and primarily in the *Historia general,* book 3, chap. 6, written of them by a serious chronicler,[12] diligent in inquiring into things, and who has been in the Isles and Tierra Firme many years.

NINTH OBJECTION

To his claim that war is more an impediment to the conversion of the Indians, that it does not help because they hate the Christians because of the harm they receive, and moreover, that the life and customs of the soldiers are such that their wickedness is sufficient for them [the Indians] to believe that the religion they follow is good, I say that the madman also hates the doctor who cures him, and the unruly boy hates the teacher who punishes him, but this fact does not negate the usefulness of one nor the other, nor should it be abandoned, as St. Augustine says in Epistle 50. And war and the soldiers are not there to convert or preach, but rather to subject the barbarians and pacify and secure the path for preaching. This is to be done by friars and clerics who live with good doctrine and example. This preaching must be accomplished with gentleness, as the Apostles did; and this is what St. Augustine says in Epistle 48: *If the unfaithful are frightened and do not receive teaching, the conquest will seem corrupt; and, likewise, if they should receive teaching and not be frightened, the antiquity of the custom would harden them and they would move more slowly down the path to well-being.*

TENTH OBJECTION

To his claim that the unfaithful cannot be forced to listen to preaching, it is a new and false doctrine and against all the others who have their opinion of it. For the Pope, himself and through others, has the power and even the obligation to preach the Gospel throughout the world, and this cannot be done if the preachers are not heeded; therefore, he has the power to force them to listen by the authority of Christ. *For when someone is given an enterprise, it is understood that they are given authority over those things that are necessary*

---

12. The reference is to Gonzalo Fernández de Oviedo y Valdés's *Historia general y natural de las Indias* (1535–48).

for its success, having first obeyed the laws of nature. And as
St. Thomas says (2nd, 2nd, q. 40, arts. 2 and 3): *The authority to which
the end belongs should make use of those things that lead to the end.*

ELEVENTH OBJECTION

Regarding his claim that by saving the lives of the innocent people
who were being sacrificed, the war was just, but that it should not be
done since one must choose the lesser evil, and that the evil in this
war is greater than the deaths of so many innocent, his lordship has
calculated wrongly, because in New Spain, according to those who
have returned from there and know of this, each year more than
twenty thousand persons were sacrificed; this figure, multiplied by
the thirty years since this sacrifice was ended would be six hundred
thousand, and in the entire conquest, I do not believe that more have
died than were sacrificed in one year. Moreover, because of this war,
the loss of infinite souls of those converted to faith, those present and
yet to come, will be avoided. And as St. Augustine says in Epistle 75,
it is a greater evil to lose one unbaptized soul than to kill innumerable men, though they be innocent. Well, this desire to reason away
the sacrifices of human victims is so beyond Christianity that even
these same Gentiles who were not barbarians nor inhumane took
it to be abominable, as Pliny writes these words in book 30, chapter 1: *In the year DCLVI, the Senate council determined that man
should not be sacrificed and publicly ended the celebration of the
strange rite in the temples,* and a bit later he says: *It is not possible
to adequately estimate how much is owed to the Romans for having
ended the phenomenon in which killing a man was very religious.*
Quintus Curtius, book 4, says this: *Some counselors also believed
that a religious practice should be remembered, one that certainly,
it seems to me, was never in the heart of the gods, and that has been
stopped in our days, that is, that a child born free was sacrificed to
Saturn; a practice that is truly more a sacrilege than a holy act,* and
so on. Plutarch also writes, in *Apotegmatis,*[13] that Gelon, the tyrant
of Sicily, having vanquished the Carthaginians, [ordered them] not to
sacrifice men: otherwise he would bring war upon them and destroy
them; and they promised not to do it. St. Augustine also writes of
this in the book *Quaestionum super judicum,* question 49. Therefore,

---

13. Probably *Apophthegmata Laconica.*

to say that ignorance is an excuse for a sin so unnatural and so abominable is beyond all reason. And the example he [the Bishop] brings, that war made to punish a few innocents should be ended if it cannot be done without punishing many more innocents, is out of the question. For in the city or town where men are sacrificed by the authority of the people, all are guilty, as all consent to it. I say harm comes to both guilty and innocent in all wars. But this is an accidental thing and against the will of the prince; therefore, when the cause is just and the end is holy, and the spirit of the prince is good, and he pardons the sins of the soldiers that are done against his wishes as much as he can, [the soldiers] harm themselves and their own souls and offend God, not the prince nor the cause. That most dignified author, [Jean] Gerson [1363–1429], says these words concerning moral standards in *De avaricia: When making wars, which are full of innumerable evils, only the interest of the Republic or the avoiding of harm to the people (notably worse than the harm that would come from the war) excuses these or the other innocents from mortal sin.* So in this war, whether it is done because of idolatry alone, or to avoid the deaths of innocents who were sacrificed, there are many more evils avoided because of the war than those that come of it, for in addition to this the deaths of many souls of those who are, and will be, converted, are avoided; this, being more than those that come from war, is what St. Augustine states in Epistle 75, where he says the death of one soul without baptism is a greater evil than killing infinite men, though they be innocent. And I repeat, regarding the ignorance that he [Las Casas] claims allows them to sacrifice men to their gods, this is a doctrine that cannot be sustained among Christians, *unless it ignores Catholic and Christian truth.* For by this same reason would all the idolatries in the world be excused, for all had that same blindness of holding some creatures as gods and honoring them with their sacrifices, which is inexcusable, as St. Paul says in Romans 1:21–23: *When they knew God, they glorified him not as God. . . . And* [they] *changed the glory of the incorruptible God into an image made like to corruptible man, and to birds,* and so on. And if these barbarians rightly defend their religion and idolatry, as he leads us to believe in the summary of his book, and the Lord Bishop clearly states in his confessional, it follows that they rightly condone and, consequently, rightly and without sin, do honor their idols, then it is a more serious sin to condone the crime than to commit it. This cannot be tolerated among Catholics, for idolatry is the gravest of all sins, as all theologians say, *and against natural reason* [*et contra rationem naturalem*]; for ignorance of natural law excuses no one, as both theologians and canonical lawyers agree. And regarding his claim that their favorable opinion toward the sacrifice of men is likely because the wisest men among them think thusly, and to this end he mentions Aristotle, I say the Philosopher did not mean by wise and prudent those who are least barbaric, but rather those who are among civil and humane peoples, as he declares in *Politica I*, speaking of barbarians. There is also the [story of] Abraham, which goes against [his opinion], for God did not let him sacrifice his son. And likewise the sacrifice of the firstborn, ordering the sacrifice of other animals and not those of men to be sacrificed, but that they be commuted, as St. Augustine deduces in the aforementioned book. To say those who denounce the faith of Christ and natural laws are not obligated to believe, this is openly against the Gospel, Mark 16:16: *He that believeth and is baptized shall be saved; but he that believeth not shall be damned,* for God condemns none for not doing that which is not obligatory.

TWELFTH OBJECTION

Regarding his claim that the intention of Pope Alexander in his bull [giving Spain jurisdiction over the western Indies in 1493] was that the Gospel would first be preached to the barbarians, and after they were made Christian they would be made subjects of the kings of Castile, not regarding the dominion of particular things, nor to make slaves of them, nor to take their lands away from them, but rather only to the supreme jurisdiction with some reasonable tribute for the protection of the faith and the teaching of good customs and good governance, and that this was also declared in another bull by [Pope] Paul III, I say the intention of Pope Alexander, clearly seen in the bull, was that the barbarians be subjected first to the kings of Castile, and afterwards be preached the Gospel. For it was done in this manner from the beginning, as ordered by the Catholic monarchs [Ferdinand and Isabella], who conformed to the intention of the Pope, His Pontiff being alive nine or ten years after he issued the bull. And knowing the manner of the conquest quite well, as all the successive popes here have known and approved, each of them even issuing bulls and authorizations and indulgences for the cathedral

churches erected there, as well as for bishoprics and monasteries. For
the bull by Paul III was given only against the soldiers who, without
authority from the prince, made slaves of these barbarians and [com-
mitted] many other crimes, and treated them like beasts, and for this
reason it says they must treat them as fellow men and neighbors,
since they [the Indians] were rational animals. So to say, as he says,
that they should not be subjected to the prince until after they are
made Christians, is beyond reason. For one should recognize that if
it is licit to subject them for one cause, for the protection of the faith
and so that they do not reject it and succumb to heresy, why would
it not be more licit for two causes? To wit: for this one [just men-
tioned], but first for another [reason] even more necessary, so they
do not impede the preaching nor the conversion of those who believe,
and to end idolatry and evil rites? I say, rather, that if a distinction
is to be made between these two approaches, it is more reasonable
to say that they should be subjected until they are preached to and
their idolatry ended, and they are converted to the Catholic faith;
and having done this, which is what the Church intends, they should
be made free and with the lordly powers they had at first. But not
to subject them at first so as to not force nor molest them, even
though they deserve to be deprived of this because of their sin and
idolatry, and after ending their idolatry and their receiving the faith,
to [then] force them and take their lands away so that they do not
reject the faith: this would be to punish them for what they have
not done, which is against divine and natural law. This would be as
if some pedantic person were to advise a pious prince to but verbally
admonish an old man for grave sins and enormous crimes, and that
he should forgive all that he did and that he should receive him into
his house as his own, and having done this, once that man had been
reformed, to advise the prince to condemn him to a life in the galleys
because of the suspicion and fear the man could cause by having
lived so badly for so long, that he easily could return to his earlier
sins. This would be one of the greatest follies imaginable, forgiving
the sins committed and punishing those that have not been done.
And I say more: to concede that after they are made Christians they
must be made subjects of the kings of Castile with their princes is to
contradict all he has said in order to avoid war. Because if the kings
of Castile have the right, as he says, to subject them in that manner after they have been made Christians, it is certain that if they

do not wish to be obedient, they may be rightly forced to it, and war
is necessary for this. Afterwards, it may justly be made on them for
a lesser cause than we have mentioned. And this contradicts all he
said earlier in his confessional. Therefore, if one carefully considers
this, and everything else the Lord Bishop writes, its aim is to prove
that all the conquests that have been done up to now, even though all
the directives have been followed, have been unjust and tyrannical,
and to confirm what he wrote in his confessional, which could more
truly be called infamous libel against our kings and nation, as it has
seemed to those on the Council of His Majesty; and to persuade the
Emperor not to make any conquest from now on, by which His Majesty would not be doing what he should, nor would he accomplish
the mandate of Christ in the propagation of the faith, as the Church
has entrusted him to do, nor would he convert those miserable people
yet to be conquered. For by not subjecting them, men at arms would
not go of their own cost to secure [the way for] the preachers, as
they have done up to this point, nor that of the King, for they have
other things to accomplish that are more necessary for his kingdom,
and even those here do not have sufficient income. And even if they
wished to pay the cost and send men, they would not find a man
who wanted to go so far, even if he were to receive thirty ducats per
month; for at this time they subject themselves to every danger and
expense for the benefit they expect from the gold and silver mines
and the help of the Indians, once subjected. And if anyone should
say that the Indians should pay the entire cost, as this is done in
their benefit, it is clear they would not do it but by force and defeat
in war, which brings us back to the beginning. And thus, the preachers would not go, and if they did, they would not permit them, but
would rather treat them as they did last year in Florida, upon those
who were sent without men at arms, because of this very belief and
urging of the Lord Bishop. And now that they are not being killed, a
hundred years of preaching would not have the same effect as fifteen
days would after making them subjects, thus having the freedom
to preach publicly and convert whomever wished, without fear of
priest or *cacique*. This is entirely to the contrary among those who
have not been made subjects. It is true the Lord Bishop has diligently worked to close all the doors of justification, and to remove all
authority upon which the justice of the Emperor is founded; and this
has presented a great opportunity to liberal men, mostly those who

read his confessional, who think and say that his entire aim has been
to tell the whole world that the kings of Castile rule over the Indies
unjustly and tyrannically; but he gives them that title so frivolously
and baselessly, by doing what he wishes with His Majesty, that he
may do him good or evil more than any other person. To conclude,
I say it is licit to subject those barbarians on the principle of ending
their idolatry and evil rites, and so that they do not impede preaching
and be converted more freely and easily, and so that after this they do
not turn and fall back into heresy, and so that their faith is confirmed
through conversation with Spanish Christians and they lose their
barbaric rites and customs.

With these answers I believe I have satisfied the objections and
arguments of the Lord Bishop and of those who share his opinion,
and that almost all of them are answered in my book [*Demócrates
segundo*] and its summary, printed in Rome, examined and approved
by the judgment of the most learned and dignified lords of the vicar
of the Pope and the master of the Holy Palace, and an auditor from
Rota, and praised by mutual agreement by many other learned men
of the Roman courts, as it would seem due to its having been printed.
This approval and concession by Alexander and confirmation by the
other pontiffs in the manner I described should be sufficient to erase
all doubt and scruple regarding the contents in print, and the book
that has been taken throughout Spain. I remit everything else to it,
as it addresses [the subject] at length.

against the treatise written by don Fray Bartolomé de las Casas,
Bishop of Chiapa, in the year 1552, entitled Destruction of the Indies,
condemning their conquest and opposing the defense of it.

Strength is a virtue according to the learned and by its own definition, and has the duty of always defending that which is just, as
Cicero says, whose thoughts compelled me to address such a controversy, quite certain of defending a just cause, just as don Fray Bartolomé de las Casas, or Cassaos, Bishop of Chiapa, a province found
on the continent in New Spain, would have been thinking when he
wrote his book entitled *Destruction of the Western Indies,* printed in
the year 1552, in which he certifies how the Spaniards discovered the
isle of Hispaniola in the year 1492, and how they went to settle it, as
it so happened. He also says how this isle is 600 leagues in circum-
ference, and addresses all the other circumventions, windward and
leeward, and [claims] that by the year 1541, 10,000 leagues of coast
had been discovered in Tierra Firme [i.e., the South American main-
land], as full of people as a beehive, where it seemed God had placed
most of humankind, according to the great number of Indians found
there, and that they were all destroyed by the tyranny and cruelty of
our conquerors. At this point it will be necessary to concede as well
as deny, following the heart [of his argument], for in this manner, as
the Philosopher says, the truth will be more clear; and if it is correct,
it will be conceded, as reason and deed are necessary in all things, as
Hugh [of St. Victor] says (*Didascalorum,* book 5), and if it is not, it
will be rejected with the strongest arguments and proofs possible.
Returning to the case, what we can concede is the time of the discovery and when the isle of Hispaniola and Tierra Firme were settled.

We reject his claim of 10,000 leagues of coast of the mainland as well as the innumerable people (the reasons for which we will see in the details here addressed), for as that which he proposes is partly wrong, it may be presumed to be so entirely. He says that 10,000 leagues of dry coast were discovered by the year 1541, and that its entirety, according to what he points out in his treatise, runs from Florida to the River Plate, making Florida a different land than what it is. He is obviously stumbling in the dark on this point, for considering the farthest reaches of Florida from the tip of the Keys, which is twenty-five degrees north, to the Plate River, at thirty-five degrees south, following the coastline with all its meanderings and a compass in hand, we find that there are no more than 2,800 [leagues] which, subtracted from 10,000, leave 7,200 leagues of land, and this fact cannot be denied, as anyone, even though they may not have sailed, will find this same number in the tide and course charts. And if we wished to add to this figure the two coasts of the North and South Seas [i.e., the Atlantic and Pacific], though he does not declare this, there are a total of 6,000 leagues, still leaving 4,000.

As to his claim of its being as full of Indians as a beehive, most know that the coastlines of the Northern Sea are almost entirely forests and jungles that they call *arcabucos* and *manglares* [i.e., rainforests and mangroves], and for good reason this land cannot be inhabited. There are two reasons: the first is the dense undergrowth, and the other is the poor quality of the land due to the lack of wind, so impeded by this high and dense undergrowth that it cannot bathe the land, nor can the rays of the sun, also denied entrance; therefore, the humidity and heavy mists are able to sicken the land. And it would not seem exaggerated to say the height and thickness of the trees also keep the sunlight from entering, and for whomever has not seen this and should doubt it, I cite Pliny, in his *Natural History*, who affirms that in parts of the Orient there are trees of such height that a crossbow shot cannot reach the tops of them, like these, so that neither the wind nor the sun have an effect. The inhabited villages are found in flat and cleared lands, and if there are any in the jungles and forests, it stands to reason the people must be ill and but few, except on the coast between Darién and Veragua [northern provinces of Panama], that had some [Indians] of such quality that they became ill and died when moved to a climate different from that of their native soil. If we carefully consider these 2,800 leagues, as we said before, we find two of the four parts of these jungles occupied in the aforementioned manner; and there are large tracts of 50, 100, and 200 leagues that are uninhabited. And note that this count includes the entire coast of Brazil, which is 660 leagues inhabited by the Portuguese, where neither the Castilians nor those who live there had anything to do in manner of conquests, as the Indians there are useless; not even the Portuguese make use of them except as captives. Taking these leagues into account, there are no more than those already referred to, and there are not even 1,000 leagues of coast that is inhabited, for all the rest is jungle and unpopulated, as our Spaniards found it; and this much is also true, that these places were not cleared of people by our Spaniards. We know that in these depopulated places, though they may have been reconnoitered, we have not set foot in them to settle, for the Spaniard does not settle or inhabit deserted lands, however healthy and rich they may be in gold and silver; he inhabits and settles where he finds Indians, though they may be poor and sickly, for without Indians for tribute, one cannot enjoy the fruits of the land, either within her veins [i.e., subterranean streams] or upon her summits; any settlement without Indians would be of no use, nor could one consider it a conquest, and if it were so called, I would argue that though there may be people who defend the land, one may believe that the forests and jungles of Tierra Firme as well as the aforementioned isles are unhealthy, and though it is true that native villages were found there, they were few, and those that were settled by our Spaniards diminished somewhat, and in some cases, disappeared altogether. This applies to the coasts, for if we examine the inlands, we will note the large numbers of natives who were (and are) there, and why they were there and why they ceased to be. But concluding with this coast being as full as "a beehive," and where he claims to have found the highest concentration of humankind, I say that in the opinion of those with experience there, it will be found to have been much less, and we will presently clarify the reasons for the decrease.

Along the coast of the Southern Sea [i.e., Pacific Ocean], which includes Peru, Tierra Firme, and New Spain, great concentrations of people were found in parts, as we will state later; other places, however, such as along the Magellan Strait to the port of Valdivia [in southern Chile], and from Esmeraldas to Bayano [northern Ecuador to Panama], and from Mariato to Cartago and Esparza [western

Panama to Costa Rica], and from the port of Concepción to the Californias and the point of St. Augustine and Cape Mendocino [northwest Mexico and Alta California], which is a great number of leagues, the Spaniards have not yet finished conquering, due to the many obstacles.

He says more: that [the Indians] are the simplest people in the world created by God, without evil or duplicity, obedient, extremely faithful, peaceful, of a fragile constitution, and who most easily perish from illness; and that they are sincere and not greedy and quite opposed to the possession of worldly goods, and with so much abstinence in their eating and sleeping that the Holy Fathers in the desert would not appear to possess more. Finally, he describes them as having so many good manners and being so virtuous that, according to our Holy Faith, there can be no doubt that any of them who had received Holy Baptism would be saved, even if he were to live many years. But to speak truly instead of with irony, and to clarify how they [i.e., the Indians] seemed to me without raising false testimony about them (as I value my salvation as much as the Bishop values his), I begin by saying that he believes them full of all virtues, where I believe they lack them. It is often said in all the Indies among contemplative people that when the Indian finds himself free and without fear, he has no virtues, but when he is subjected and fearful, he appears to possess all of them. This must be why I, having always dealt with free and fearless Indians, in peace and in war, have found them to be completely lacking any sort of virtue, as I have said; whereas on the contrary, the Bishop dealt with the servants in his monasteries, forced into service for many years; and so it is that those who frequent the monasteries, like it or not, are neither idolatrous nor bellicose, and if they had been, they either hide it or have lost it through Christian and religious communion, demonstrating the notable humility with which they repress the many vices they have. I would like to know whether the Bishop entered that land alone and before the conquests in order to preach the Holy Gospel to them, and whether he found them to be as humble as he proclaims. If he were alive, he would tell me that he had not attempted it; and I am certain that if he had, they would have been full of virtue in the [form of] flesh from his own body, and if they did not eat human flesh, I am certain they would have at least killed him with a million torments, making a bridge with his body over the swamps and streams, as has already been witnessed, having found some priests who bravely and piously offered themselves unto martyrdom in order to preach the Holy Gospel to them. To give proof of some of the places where they [i.e., priests] have been found made into bridges, I mention Carare, in the province of El Sollo [in New Granada], on the banks of the great Magdalena River; and this is not an unusual thing, for it has happened in all parts of the Indies, or at least most of them.

And because it serves our purpose, one may note what happened [on the coast of Venezuela] in Cumaná and Cumanagoto when the blessed Bishop, as a cleric, came to Spain in order to persuade and pester His Majesty the Emperor Charles V, of glorious memory, with lengthy explanations and persuasions baptized in holy examples, to give him unarmed laborers along with their wives and children, so that they might settle [among] those Indians, who were but lambs, and to remove Gonzalo de Ocampo and his soldiers who were settled there, accusing these of being cruel; for if they were to enter the land, not with severity and stratagems of war, but with good will and simple welfare, the Indians would be quite content and servile, and would attempt no betrayal as they had at other times, and they would observe the peace. And His Majesty, though he should have seen differently, and so that no kind of severity would be attributed to him, made use of his usual clemency and conceded this to [Las Casas] and gave him the commission, ships, and provisions. He gathered the people and they embarked and arrived at the coast and stepped ashore, taking complete possession of it and removing the captain and the people who lived in the town (who left quite certain of what would happen afterwards), and there he was, making himself known to the Indians with many gifts. He settled (or rather unsettled) the land while the Indians waited for them to rest a few days and recover from the desolate sea. And seeing that they had regained their weight, the Indians gathered and cruelly attacked them, killing them and eating most of them (and this happened at the same time that the sincere Bishop was at the Royal Audiencia [high court] in Santo Domingo negotiating for his republic). But at this time there was no lack of people to imitate the religious ceremonies, bringing the breviary by hand, for all [the Indians] wore the clothes and dresses of the villagers, taking the place of their owners; they made a thousand martyrs of them and their wives, so grave that when [the soldiers] went to punish them, they found the villagers rotting on the beaches with horns stuck in their lower parts, and this would have been after making [sexual] use of them. All these people died, and not a creature escaped.[14]

I have presented this occurrence as an example of the harm that ignorance causes, even though it is wrapped in holy appearances; and if it is true that the person who provokes a crime is as guilty as the one who commits it, the Bishop was guilty, for this occurrence is why he took up his Dominican habit and returned to Spain, where he wrote the treatise referred to, later becoming the Bishop of Chiapa. And I say he was guilty of this deed, for because of him this settlement was brought to so much pain, assuring goodness where there was none, nor has any been seen in the natives of those parts, for if there are any cruel people in the world, they are these, by the experience we have with the things they attempt and do, as we will later demonstrate. It is natural to find cruelty in cowardly spirits, for they are as cowardly as they are cruel, as Aristotle said, depraved as wild beasts, and these Indians show this well; and it is born from this: when they find themselves defeated and afraid, they are lambs; but when they need it, and are given freedom with victory, there are no tigers so fierce.[15] And so, if they turn to obedience and the doctrine of the Holy Gospel, it is because they see the strength of the soldiers. Up to now, the religious have had no effect upon them in the Western Indies, entering the land alone and with no armed support; there have been many attempts and their lives are lost. If there has been any [effect], it is among Indians who are tired of war and ready for peace and who see armed soldiers close by. I will give my opinion as a man who has had so much experience and has dealt so much with them in the conquests and in peace and, believe me as the Christian I am, that in order to convert them both the religious and the warriors must enter the land together so that their conversion is made brief and more souls are saved, for, according to St. Bernard, there is nothing in this whole world more esteemed than even one [soul]. And if some

14. For a clearer sense of Las Casas's failed 1519–20 Venezuelan colony, which Vargas Machuca has here distorted, see the Introduction.

15. On the so-called tiger spirit of the mainland Caribs, see, for example, Neil L. Whitehead, "The Snake Warriors—Sons of the Tiger's Teeth: A Descriptive Analysis of Carib Warfare, 1500–1820," in *The Anthropology of War*, ed. Jonathan Haas (Cambridge: Cambridge University Press, 1990), and *Dark Shamans: Kanaimà and the Poetics of Violent Death* (Durham: Duke University Press, 2002).

Indians are found to be of a laudable condition, they should be highly regarded, treating them well and with honor as is done between virtuous and noble allies, whom the conqueror will recognize, favorably received with assured peace, because with such extraordinary manners and natures, extraordinary effects are certain.

First Discourse and Defense
in favor of the Conquest
of the Isle of Hispaniola.

The Devil's malice ordinarily seeks to take reason from humans so that they are converted into brute animals, and it is in this way that he has possessed these Indians such a long time and this is easily seen in what the very same Bishop of Chiapa writes in his *Treatise on the Isle of Hispaniola,* in which they imagined Spaniards to be children of the sun, and when they discovered that they were not, they fled into the jungles, where they ended as barbarians; and I confess this is true. In addition to this, he says the cruelties done to them by the Spaniards were innumerable, charging them first with eating the provisions of the fugitives while obligating the rest to give them their usual rations; and likewise in the uprisings, [accusing them of] causing great harm, killing a hundred [Indians] for each one of ours killed by them, so that in time most, if not all, of them came to a miserable end. He also tells of five powerful kingdoms on the isle of Hispaniola, omitting the innumerable and inferior others. He says more: that the Spaniards used dogs in order to finish them off, fattening [the dogs] on them and cruelly tearing them apart. He says more: that they took advantage of the women of the [native] lords, dishonoring and offending them, whose sense of honor was such that the Indians abhorred them and they went into the jungles and forests to die. As to that which is here referred to, some points may be conceded, but everything else is denied and we proceed by giving sufficient reasons on particular points and in general, such that all which follows will be correct, having made this defense and the principle upon which it is founded.

As for their imagining that the Spaniards are children of the sun and that man and horse are one, this has generally been true, at first sight, in all of the Indies, and the same occurs in the new conquests.

From this one may well understand their barbarity, as they neither made nor make discourse about nor consider the division of the two bodies. And if they were seen as humble, submissive, obedient, and servile it is because of this imagination and apprehension they had, as well as the fear caused by the furious horses and frightening thundering of the harquebuses [early handguns], appearing as cruel lightning bolts from the heavens. But in time, discovering the truth and realizing [the Spaniards] were mortal men, subject to die as they themselves were, they lost all respect and that initial obedience, gathering the courage to take up arms against our men, and forging in their malice diverse betrayals, putting into execution all they could; and those that had no effect had none because they were discovered and punished in time, stopping their evil intentions. But those who have succeeded have caused inhumane cruelties, setting Spanish towns afire, first burning the churches and the Holy Sacrament within, making martyrs of the religious with many and varied torments and deaths, eating them cooked and boiled, taking many men and women whose eyes were torn out to dance in their drunken revelries and gatherings on leashes they attach through a hole pierced under the lower jaw. Some of these are fattened up in order to be eaten, and others guard the crops from the parrots, shouting all day from atop high platforms made of four poles and suffering this cruel torment until they die. Others are burned and made into ash in order to drink in *chicha*, which is a wine they make.[16] They make war flutes of the bones and eat on plates made of the crowns of the skulls, triumphant. In effect, at every turn they are the most cruel people in the world, as brutish as they are cruel, and it is my opinion (and that

16. Vargas Machuca seems to be referring in this last charge to mortuary cannibalism. On this practice in the Amazon, see Beth Conklin, *Consuming Grief: Compassionate Cannibalism in an Amazonian Society* (Austin: University of Texas Press, 2001). The other charges—for example, gouging out captives' eyes, or making them guard crops from parrots—are recited in Vargas Machuca's *Indian Militia*, where they are attributed to the Pijaos of New Granada's upper Magdalena and Cordillera Central (113). The practice of running a rope through the captive's lower jaw (among other humiliations and tortures) was assigned to the alleged Caribs inhabiting the middle Magdalena during the early conquest wars. Description of this torture, suffered by the son of conquistador Pedro de Añasco, had become a kind of trope by Vargas Machuca's time, as it shows up in both Juan de Castellanos's ca. 1592 epic poem, *Elegías de varones ilustres*, and Fray Pedro Simón's 1625 *Noticias historiales de las conquistas de Tierra Firme en las Indias Occidentales*, 9 vols. (Bogotá: Biblioteca de Autores Colombianos, 1953).

of many who have dealt with them) that in order to paint a perfect picture of cruelty one must but paint a portrait of an Indian.[17]

As for their dealings and communication, it is true they do not tell the truth, nor have ever known how to keep faith, nor word, nor promise with those who have trusted them. One is forced to believe they are a people with neither honor nor esteem, and this truth is verified by knowing for certain that they sell wife, daughter, and sister to any Spaniard to make dishonest [i.e., carnal] use of; one may infer from this that they are a people with no reason, depraved and without honor. Without this, virtue cannot be sustained, for a sense of shame is its most important foundation; as Plato says, honor is a dignity acquired with virtue, such that it is the mother of honor and forms a substantial part of its very definition (the definition that Aristotle gives affirms this argument and favors my cause), for virtue is that which creates all that is good. As all of their acts are evil, it follows that they have no honor, and whoever should lack this lacks virtue as well; and of peoples who lack both, one may consider which it might be. I know not why I tire myself with presenting the material further, as we know that those who eat human flesh eat their own children and vassals; and so that their barbarity may be seen, I can say that they disobey and break the laws of nature itself, which normally incline one to the conservation of man and to desire a long life and flee from death; they, voluntarily and for slight causes, hang themselves. One may believe that a people who do this are without faith and without God, and I say this not only of the true Creator, but even of the false gods; if they had any faith, it would be recognized, for, as Plato says, man is a royal possession and property of this same God, to whom injury is done when one takes his own life, as the slave would do to his master, killing himself against his [master's] will.

Not only that, they are even more brutish than irrational animals, for we see that these procure to feed and preserve their species and there are none that do not love and care for their children, placing their lives in danger so that they may live, and these indomitable savages go against the universal law of nature, wishing to destroy themselves; and to prevent their descendants from being obligated

17. Martínez de Salinas Alonso's transcription reads: "in order to definitively *end* cruelty [*para quitar la crueldad*] . . . one must but *kill* an Indian [*matar un indio*]" (Vargas Machuca, *Apologías y discursos,* 64). Neither the Salamanca manuscript nor the Royal Palace transcription of 1879 shows this variation.

to heed doctrine and serve the Spaniards, they drown the females at birth; and this has sometimes been observed in the provinces of the Panches and Colimas [now extinct Carib-speaking peoples of the middle Magdalena River just west of Bogotá] and in many others. Finally, though they may have been baptized, most of them are idol-worshipers and speak with the Devil, and according to their inclination it may be understood that they will die as they have lived. All this and many other things of no lesser gravity I will not speak of, so as to not tire nor be thought of more as one impassioned rather than a true author.

And the Bishop kept silent about this because his primary intention was to give credit to them, blaming the Spaniard for cruelty and tyranny; and to the legal punishments that we are addressing he gave the unjust name of cruelties without considering nor admitting their causes nor the motive of the Spaniards; for many things are poorly judged that are not clearly seen nor well understood from the beginning. And what happened to a cleric of one of those provinces confirms this.

Wanting his parishioners to learn and love evangelical doctrine and observe it with Christian zeal, [this cleric] brought the cruel sorrows of Purgatory to their minds in a sermon. And after extolling what he could, he said that he would demonstrate them to whoever wished to see. At this point two curious, or rather garrulous, Indians asked the priest to show them and so the good cleric tied them to a pole that was set in the ground for a pillory or gibbet, and made a circle of firewood around them, two paces away. It must have been well made, because of the effect. He set it afire all around with the spirit and intention that he would tear the wood from the circle and untie them when it became too hot. He did this, but was unable to undo it, for when he tried to save them it was too late, or he was prevented, or the Devil stoked the fire so that the Indians died. The archbishop of this place, knowing the case, sent for the imprisoned priest and pardoned him for his simplicity, knowing it had not been done with malice, but with pure innocence. After having taken the measures required by the case, [the priest] returned to his parish and priesthood with a just punishment. This well-known occurrence was no cruelty, as it is clear this incident passed before a learned and Christian tribunal. Who doubts that whoever might be told of this deed, that a priest tied two Indians up and surrounded them with firewood and lit them on fire and burned them, would say that it was a great cruelty? However, telling it with its circumstances he would not say so, but would instead recognize it as ignorance.

He charges that the Spaniards ate the provisions of the Indians and forced them to sustain the Spanish republic [i.e., settler community], and not being able to do so, [the Indians] fled in fear to the jungles and forests, where great numbers of them died. This offence is satisfied by natural law, for in times of necessity and gravity such as our men suffered at that time, goods are common and are to be made use of as if they were one's own; there was no quick rescue they could hope for, nowhere to buy [provisions], and none of the provisions they had when they set sail from Spain, which were not to last so long as to assuage hunger on land, and so it was necessary to sustain themselves and make the Indians bring them supplies. But because it was in so strange a place and so mysterious and unknown to them, it was just and necessary to have compelled them to it, for as Seneca says, man defeats all things but hunger. [The Indians] are of such quality and nature that they place themselves in danger of losing their lives to hunger because they do not work, eating fruits and wild roots when the labors in the fields are doubled in order to sustain their guests; and it is believed that the Spaniards, while they wished to work with their hands, understood neither the art nor the seasons of the land, and so it was justified to force [the Indians] to enlarge their fields, and they do it to this day though they are better Christians and friends, for if the *encomendero* in charge of the administration of a village does not do this or does not mete out justice, neither the republic of the Spaniards nor that of the Indians could be sustained as it is.[18]

I would like to know what blame the Spaniard and justice should have if these idlers rebel every day, hiding in the jungles, eating and surviving on wild fruits and roots as mentioned. They are of such a condition that when they rebel and become fugitives they burn their own houses and cut down the crops and fruit trees they have in their fields, determined to die in the wild and prevent the Spaniard from making use of them. And it is true that if they move to a different climate, however little distance that may be in those parts, even two

18. The reference is to the legally separate communities established by the Spanish crown in the Americas: the *república de españoles* and the *república de indios*.

or four leagues, they later fall ill and die miserably, and here is the reason that in hot lands and sea coasts the Indians have wasted away: first, because of the poor disposition and sickness of the land, and second, because they trust that it is hot land, so wherever they spend the night they may do so with water and a palm heart, but though this is sweet and tasty, it is pestilent. Also, in places such as these their dwellings are divided; this does not happen in cold lands as they are congregated in native communities [*repúblicas*] where they may recover; and they do not dare abandon their houses not only because of this, but also so that others cannot occupy them, fearing the cold. And since the lands are cold and lacking in wild foods, the Indians are better workers, and in these lands they have survived and prospered in such a manner that we will prove there are even more of them today than when the Spaniards entered, as we will later give evident reasons. It is true that some in hot lands have survived, but with such little work they have wasted away, generally because of the quality of hot lands in addition to the other illnesses they encounter.

He also charges that the Spaniards take the wives and daughters away from the caciques, abusing them and using them for manual work. To this I respond with a well-known truth, that the Indian customs in matrimony always were a tacit agreement and conformity of wills, without any further ceremony, using this liberty to have up to twenty or thirty wives, and among them there are often a sister, a cousin, or a daughter, and all are abused, even the mother. All of the women serve and respect the one who is most loved and each night [the caciques] choose whom they will sleep with. Well, considering thirty women married to only one man, and that among them there is only one who is desired while the rest are scorned, it is no surprise that they lay eyes upon the Spaniards, and freely solicit and provoke them. Therefore, it is not such a guilty crime that an incited man attends to her intentions; it is a different thing for a man to receive a woman in his house than if he goes to take her from hers; and if the priest or Spanish encomendero takes one into the service of his house, it is no great offense, as the cacique has so many to serve him, he will not miss one. This, however, rarely happens, and if the cacique is married according to our religion, it is a sure and true thing that there is no encomendero or soldier who would have knowingly taken his wife. But if this cacique or other Indian has another dozen women more than the one given by the hand of the priest, among them the

sister, daughter, or cousin with whom he sleeps with no respect for
God or the one who is legitimate, it would be meritorious to take her
and separate her from him. But there is the problem that there are
many encomenderos who ignore this and take no such action so as
not to offend their caciques; and I know of some who are worthy of
great punishment for ignoring this, for those who permit this are as
guilty as the one who commits the act. As for saying [the Spaniards]
take their children, I do confess this, although this also rarely happens; one should first blame the encomenderos, for they generally do
this with little care; however, they should be permitted to do it, as a
million benefits would come of it. First, [the children] are well indoc-
trinated in the house of the Spaniard, in our Holy Faith as well as in
all the other customs; second, they are well dressed and cared for; and
third, they learn the Spanish language and become accustomed to the
Spaniards in such a way that they themselves call their parents and
family barbarous. Because of these servants and children, Spaniards
have discovered great rebellions planned by the Indians and have
averted them in time so they could not succeed. Likewise, if the son
of the cacique and lord inherits [anything], he leaves the house of the
encomendero with great respect and courtesy, and it is a certain thing
that they govern their people better, making them friendly to the
Spaniards, showing how much they are indebted to them, and I have
heard it from them myself on occasion, and few who have been in the
Indies can deny that if the Spaniards had not gone to that land, all [of
the Indians] would be condemned as idol-worshipers and savages; and
apart from this they would not know anything of decorum, such as
riding a horse or being well dressed, nor would they have such good
and abundant provisions, nor the art of song and music, reading and
writing, and knowing how to wield a sword, nor would they know
how to paint so curiously, nor work silver and gold, nor the other arts
and professions, nor any of the other educated and urbane customs;
this occurs often among Indians who attain some sort of thankfulness and nobility, for good works are tied to noble hearts and as
St. Augustine says (*Soliloquid* 18), thankfulness must be as great as
the benefit received. This is the harm the Spaniards cause when they
take the children into their service, as the Bishop of Chiapa exaggerates. If it is a girl, when her parents ask to marry her off, the encomendero is pleased by this goodness, because the manners, Christian
communication, and good customs and practices that she carries with

her, having learned them from her governess, are thereby passed to
the other Indian girls.

He also charges that they mistreat the Indians, punishing them,
and this I do concede to him, but not the intention with which he
claims. He refers to it as severe cruelty where it is none other than
fraternal punishment and correction, and this is not usually done
by all the Spaniards, but rather by the administrator, their encomendero, who is responsible for them. And if this is guilt, it is the
same into which fall the friars and cleric priests, since they and their
agents punish their observance of doctrine with zeal, whose severity
commands the respect of their poor inclination; and they are punished for fleeing (even as Christians), and because they stop attending services during celebrations, and because they do not send their
children to services morning and afternoon during the week, as is
customary, taking them away instead so they do not attend. And it
has happened that a priest had been teaching doctrine for two years
when he happened upon some Indian boys and girls who had been
hidden away all that time. At other times they are punished because
of complaints by their caciques that they are disobedient and they do
not dare punish them; and others for mistreating their mothers and
daughters, lying down with them, and also for things no less blame-
worthy, such that finally their poor behavior and lack of Christianity
require severity. Well, if the missionary priests so pious are permitted to punish them, why are their encomenderos and administrators
charged and blamed for these same reasons and just causes, if they
have at any time laid hands upon them? Are they not responsible
for them and held accountable to the same obligations when such
crimes are brought to their attention, [even] if they are unable to
pursue justice, upon which the governance and order of their town
depend because it is far away and remote, and thereby prevent other
crimes, great or small? And so it is not so great a thing if sometimes,
moved to anger and incited by the liberties and depraved things that
are committed in their presence, they rough them up a bit. And it is
no important thing, for in Spain this is often done to house servants,
but only by the encomendero administrator with no one else daring
to, nor the Indians allowing it, for they know well how to exaggerate their complaint for justice, as we have seen; and we know that
if they receive a blow from anyone, they give themselves more,
striking themselves in the nose so that the blood runs. They spread it

over their face, shirt, and garments, and in this state they go seeking justice, making a great fuss and a thousand gestures, for they are extremely inventive. And the Spaniard, in order not to be troubled with the justice sought in this manner by the Indian, concedes to him, paying him in gold or blankets, as that is their manner of clothing, for the Indian wants nothing more than to satisfy his greed. His accusation is not made in order to punish the Spaniard whom he accuses of the offense, but rather he aspires only for pay; they would sell their daughters and wives out of greed for money or clothing or another thing of value, and this goes well with what the Bishop claims, that they are not greedy. They are so much so that before God I say that it has happened to me, walking through a peaceful land, that I have arrived at a crossroads not knowing which way to follow. Asking a nearby Indian which path to take, he responded, "Daca paga [Pay me]." And I am quite certain that there are but few Spaniards who have wandered these parts to whom the same has not occurred. Well, I wonder if there is any human greed in the world so great that they even wish to sell benevolence, something no other nation does, rather being moved to compassion for the one who does not know and asks, responding graciously and showing him the way. In such a situation, it seems to me that if this were to happen to an honorable Spaniard who does not know the way he is to take, it would be correct if he, being somewhat phlegmatic, were to pay for his guidance and statements, or being choleric, to charge at him with his horse and run him down and force him to tell him regardless and, so that he does not lie or lead him astray, to grab him and make him serve as a guide until they should happen upon someone who can assure that he is going in the right direction.

Concerning their possessions and food, if a Spaniard arrives in need and without money and asks for some necessary thing, I know well that they will not give anything voluntarily without pay regardless of how necessary it is, unless the Spaniard is not already determined to take it away by force, at which time they are silent and let him carry it off; and concerning this there is no one in the Indies who would not confess all of this to be true; and they are commonly referred to as being a cunning people for these and worse things. It is taken for certain that the Devil has ordered them to commit these graceless deeds and worse customs. Lacking good communication with the Spaniard, they will not follow our Holy Faith correctly, and they have made promises to him [i.e., the Devil] and follow his orders, as they often talk with him. The Devil is so perverse that he may neither do nor speak nor imagine good, and we suppose that he must always deceive us into being pleased with his actions. And so we see that the Indian will not forget the evil done to him unless it is because of one of two things: either fear of the person who does it, or greed, and when it is greed and not fear, they have an infinity of lies. And so that one may see what they are, I will tell of a thing that happened in the city of Trinidad, in the province of the Muzos in the New Kingdom of Granada, as proof.

And it so happened, while [I served as] governor in that place and province, that a newly arrived gentleman who still lives there named Juan Juárez de Cepeda, servant of Alonso Ruiz Lanchero, an encomendero and conqueror of that province and city, apparently struck or kicked an Indian twice, and there was nothing more [to it], according to the evidence in the case. The Indian, having taken the bit in the teeth, was so troubled that he had three or four family members carry him to the house of the governor, feigning his death. [The effect] was so extreme that the governor was greatly alarmed and took the ordinary and extraordinary actions to revive his Indian, but was unable, the body appearing pale, the eyes turned back, the limbs dislocated and the arms and legs in such a state that they remained in whatever position they were placed, all of which so confused the governor that he resolved to arrest the encomendero and his servant, the aggressor. Once captured, he began proceedings against them with great rigor, and looking further into the case, had a doctor summoned, who, upon carefully examining [the Indian] and turning him here and there, found his pulse to be normal. Having been assured that he was not dead, the governor used precisely the right stratagem to reveal the trickery and lie. Before employing it, however, he spoke to the Indian, offering that if he were to regain consciousness, he would order the encomendero to give him and his wife a gift of clothing of some importance. And sending for some food, wine, and a bowl of seasoned broth, he poured it into his mouth and [the Indian] coughed it up and drooled like a dead person. Seeing that his efforts were in vain, he used his first idea, which was to set a handful of straw on fire and bring it close to the Indian who, when he felt it, gave a howl, stood up, and began to flee, but he was not so fleet as to not be caught. The indignant governor justly whipped him and cut off his hair, punishing his accomplices in the ruse as well, having [falsely] accused and testified that [Cepeda's] steward had beat him to death with a club. The doctor, upon examining [the case], found no evidence of this whatsoever. This same governor had been told of administrators in some places who had killed Indians in punishing them and had buried them. They swore to this and indicated where; and when he sent constables and scribes with them they found no one, even when they dug up the earth, and they later were found to have fled and the "buried" were fugitives. Once this trickery was verified, he punished the informers and false witnesses, and serving them justice he was able to prevent similar testimonies and lies. Finally, in this manner he discovered and brought the truth to light, preventing a million treacheries, appearances, and deceptions; as St. Augustine says, malice and evil cannot blossom long, just as lies and deceits soon return to their natural states.

The same occurred several times to Dr. Salazar, the longest-serving president of the Royal Audiencia of that kingdom [of New Granada], dead Indians being brought into his presence because of abuses by Spanish soldiers, and being revived, a brave and habitual custom of theirs. The truth, naked of all deception or lies, has never been observed in this people, and they will continue this way as long as they follow the Devil with their idolatries and sacrifices, often hanging and killing themselves for him. Another notable thing that furthers our purpose occurred to this same governor, having been advised by the Royal Audiencia of Santa Fe [in New Granada] that a judge named Doctor Francisco Guillén was coming to audit the government and punish the excesses that had been committed against the Indians, fulfilling royal will and letters patent. He noticed a house in the city that seemed to him a comfortable place to stay, and in order to provide the best and most spacious hospitality, its owner, named Marmolejo, took his entire family to a nearby Indian village where he was encomendero, leaving a room in the kitchen to an Indian servant girl so that she would keep the house and cook for the new guest. It so happened that when the judge and [royal] visitor was moving into the house, the girl hanged herself in her room; when they went looking for her to put the kitchen in order, they found her already dead and hanging from a beam. The [royal] visitor was so upset by this scandal that he thought he would lose his sense of judgment, considering that he was to punish apparent excesses caused by the encomenderos and he saw with his very eyes just how such a spectacle occurred. He quickly sent for the governor and once he arrived, ordered him to pursue the case and bring justice. The governor answered that he would do it with great care, but of the royal visitor, being such a learned man, he begged to know against whom he should bring his case, if it was to be against the master who left her to guard the house and provide hospitality to him, or against [the judge himself] who received it, or against the Indian girl who hanged herself so as not to welcome new people, or against the conqueror or settler of the city. The judge and visitor was left so confused by all this that the case is unresolved to this day, and I doubt that the Bishop could resolve it (even though he would record it as a cruelty). And who would not judge it so, if it were written simply that this Indian girl hanged herself in the house of her Spanish encomendero without telling the case as it happened, as [the Bishop] writes of all the cruelties he claims and tells of in his treatise, not including the circumstances and reasons behind them?

This case opened the eyes of the judge, though a newcomer to the land, considering all those he had the opportunity to punish, and how, upon closely examining things, he found very little blame on the part of the Spaniards, or on the part of the governor who was a great gentleman and Christian, experienced and skilled in the land, as well as an example of the many deceptions and cunning that the Indians had wished to use with him as with all who govern the Indies. And if I do not present them as evidence in this matter, knowing the ruses, tricks, wiles, lies, and deceptions of the Indians, there is no one who will give them credit as being reasonable discourse, and I trust God that those who should finish reading this proof will find that the deception of the Bishop is clear.

The First Defense Continues
further declaring the charges the Bishop makes against the conquerors, and responding to them with satisfactory rejoinder.

According to St. Chrysostom, deception always has a fine appearance, and the Bishop was behind it in the accusations made to him by impassioned and aggrieved hearts, accusing the conquering soldiers, when punishing, of killing a hundred Indians for every Spaniard killed, and that in their vengeance they take delight in nothing but cruelties, stabbing them to death and having dogs trained and fed in order to tear them apart, hanging some and impaling others, and that [the Indians] flee from the harquebuses in terror, finally perishing miserably. Here is a response to what he says regarding their repaying the differences in deaths one hundred to one, baptized in cruelties, from which the terrified Indians flee and are finished off by the harquebuses.

As to the first point, I confess that a hundred to one die when [the soldiers] go to carry out a punishment and [the Indians] do not surrender the criminals, for if they did, it is certain that none other than the aggressor would die, even though, astonishingly, they are killing Spaniards. They do not even burn a church without having first made council with all the land and her principal men, or the cacique who would do it with all of his subjects, none of whom are excluded from the conspiracy and drunken revelry. And as they are all in on the deed, they all support it, risking their lives with weapons in hand, as they have all promised this before taking up arms and breaking the peace. And precisely when news of any uprising that has occurred reaches the responsible audiencia or governor, commission is immediately given to a commander and his soldiers to defeat and pacify [the land's inhabitants], ordering him to judiciously castigate the guilty party. This they do to the guilty and they do it with incredible brevity, for if there were any delay in the dispatch, the damage that the Indians cause is irreversible, as we have already seen on many and diverse occasions, and as it is said that danger lies in delay, with swiftness it is harmlessly avoided. These officers depart and find the land in rebellion, villages burned, and the Spaniards in them dead or hanged or already eaten, if [the Indians in those parts] eat human flesh, leaving the bodies without legs or arms, which are what they crave, strewn over the ground; and as proof of the crime

the dwellings of the Spaniards are torn down and destroyed, their
Spanish-speaking servants dead, leaving no dog or cat with life and
the horses and other livestock shot through with arrows. Upon
witnessing such deeds, the commander or officer makes his judgment
and procedure and, once completed, follows the trail and path by
which [the Indians] retreated, for at that point it is useless to [simply]
make a public accusation, which is why they search them out, looking
over their shoulders, in order, and arms at the ready; for the Indians
are quite vigilant in times of war, such that wherever the soldiers
tread, they count their steps in order to discover their preparedness
and intention; and if they are able to defeat them hand-to-hand,
they take no precaution, attacking them with many ambushes, using
various stratagems. They try to do this by night, unnoticed, and
if this is not possible and they have enough people, they attack by
day and on open ground, and they fight until one band is seen to be
defeated (though this happens rarely with some caciques), for unless
all the land acts together in the uprising, they are careful to retreat
where they cannot be found or chanced upon. As St. Ambrose says,
there is no safe place for the infidel or traitor, so during these retreats
they make through ill and uninhabitable lands with no food: all of
them suffer and perish; and as hunger takes them, if they eat human
flesh (as we have mentioned), the cacique often kills the people so
that he and his subjects may eat and sustain themselves while their
hunger lasts.

These are the cruelest tyrants, preferring to eat each other and to
perish rather than to guard and keep the peace because of their vile
inclination and nature; this, as well as what I have said before God,
is true, for aside from having occurred to many other commanders
and their expeditions, it happened to me. In the city of the Muzos, in
the very same Kingdom of [New] Granada, a cacique named Guazara rebelled with all his people and subjects; and after much death
and destruction, he fled through great and expansive forests, some
uninhabited and some inhabited by warring savages called Carares.
I gathered my men and departed to reduce and punish him [Guaz-
ara], and after more than two months of searching for and following
him, we came upon him by way of a remarkable strategy (having
nothing to do with our purpose here). As soon as I recognized him,
he was attacked, and within one hour he and many of his men were
defeated and taken prisoner. I questioned him and verified that he

and the people who followed had killed and eaten more than forty of the most unnecessary men and women; I found much of this flesh preserved in salt, and by my faith, I found and witnessed an entire Indian wrapped in *bihao* leaves and roasted on a *barbacoa*, which is like a great rack raised on legs made of young wood with coals below; he could not be eaten because of my assault. And if one considers that in one and a half months or two since the skirmish they had eaten forty people, in one or two years they would finish off all his people and all his subjects. In the end, with his punishment, the present damages were remedied and those to come were prevented, and this is how most of his people came to be converted as they are today, for the rest were diminished by the sickness that overcame them in those deserts before I found them, and afterwards, in the fight, some were found missing as is ordinary in battles and skirmishes. In this way, many perish and die, seeking their own deaths, without the Spaniard being the primary cause, as the Bishop claims, but rather by their own fault. Our desire is none other but to have security and peace in the provinces we inhabit, and rational men do not find this difficult to believe; we know that even irrational brutes keep the peace and delight in it, especially those who possess the necessary understanding and discourse to know the certain and indubitable truth that Titus Livy says, that a secured peace is better than a victory merely hoped for. And as St. Augustine says (Epistle 5): cities are beautified and maintained with peace and accord, but with discord they are destroyed and perish. No Spaniard should cease from considering and knowing for certain the benefit gained by making peace with the natives, for in this way they enjoy a safe life and have property and peace, but if the land rebels they lose these three things only to gain immense labors, hunger and excessive heat, fatigue and weariness, and without this, which is unbearable, continuous danger, sickness, injury, and death.

It is common knowledge that the Spaniard neither desires nor seeks war, as the Indian does, constantly instigating betrayals and uprisings, committing robberies and murders by burning churches and towns, as we have said and will continue to show. That a hundred Indians die for every Spaniard they kill, as the Bishop says, is not such a great thing. And I wish to confess this, however, one must understand and consider the manner this occurs, so that our Spaniards are saved from guilt. It is true that in those places the life of one Spaniard is esteemed so highly, for there are so few of them against so many, and this [life] must be protected so as to not lose what has been built. Considering this, when it happens that one or many are killed during peace, the punishment is meted out with such consideration that if a hundred [Indians] justly deserve death, not more than one or two receive it, because if the lives of the Indians are not protected as well, there will be none to settle, and the land without them is of no use to the Spaniard, as we will demonstrate below. But if before surrendering to this punishment the Indians defend themselves with armed resistance and a hundred to one die in the following defeat and flight because of the harquebuses, how can the Spaniards be blamed for this? I believe it is by divine permission that such a great number die because of the great harm they cause his Divine Majesty, for the Spaniard is never severe outside of armed conflict, but rather shows himself pious, sociable, and a friend both to the one who has surrendered and the one who still has not, always maintaining reason, justice, and Christianity, following the words of St. Gregory, for he who does pious deeds knows to first protect justice, since faith is a degree of piety; this being true, the Christian can be nothing less than pious, obligated with this respect to proceed with justice when meting out punishment, charging the principal aggressors under the terms of the law, albeit more swiftly according to the customs of war and the brevity of time, providing for their defense and, if they are judged guilty and deserving death, condemning them to it. And no one to this day has been given [death] that was not first convicted of the crime. And if it is said that executing them by impalement is a great cruelty, I confess it is true that in some provinces they have carried out this manner of punishment, as in others that of hanging; but if one considers the manner in which they are impaled, we find the punishment is not excessive, for they are first garroted. Furthermore, in our Spain, when they have hanged someone, they are quartered and each part is put on a pole; but in the wars in those places, so as not to stop to quarter a body, or wander around in the hills looking for so many poles, they are put on one. It is true that in some parts they have been impaled alive and then shot with arrows or [balls from a] harquebus, but these Spaniards were incited to vengeance by seeing their wives and children and relatives killed and eaten with incredible inhumanity. This happens when they are not baptized and wish to die as idolaters invoking the Devil. And this crime could be as scandalous and cruel as, in Spain, when they are placed in a barrel alive[19] or tortured with tongs and shot with arrows, and in France they burn them and put them on a wheel, breaking their legs and arms while alive, and in Germany and Flanders they give other, even more severe deaths, [whereas] in the Indies, in some parts during wartime these punishments have been used, but it has been on very rare occasions, and if [the Indians] were to be punished in accordance to the cruelties they themselves use, I believe using tongs on them would be a minor thing.

But the Spaniards do not do this, both by being pious by nature and by fearing the justice of God and their king, and if they have been excessive they have done so in secret, for if justice knew of it they would be punished, and if such a deed committed by a few soldiers in war deserves punishment, the commanders themselves are responsible for punishing. And I confess that at some times commanders see things that seem cruel to them but that they cannot remedy, for on many occasions they take along Indian allies who go armed to aid our men, and these commit blatant acts of cruelty that the Spaniards are neither guilty of nor able to prevent, because they would rebel and become a risk. To prove this, even though I refer to it in the book *The Indian Militia*,[20] I will tell of a case that I myself condemned as inhumane.

Having gone out to punish, by order of the Royal Audiencia of Santa Fe in the New Kingdom of Granada, for some days I pursued some Indians who had rebelled, sacking the lands, killing and capturing Indian servants, burning the villages, and carrying away more than a hundred captives. We caught up with them, giving resistance and fighting, when a skirmish ensued in which the Indian allies, around 150 lancers, fought so well that the enemy was defeated, captured, and killed within two hours. As I was moving through the fray, I came upon an Indian who was holding one of the enemy on the ground and was cutting his throat like a butcher, drinking the blood as it spilt. I found his face and hands so bloodied that I severely reprehended him as being inhumane, to which he replied with pious

19. *Encubar.* Some severe crimes were punished in Spain by sealing the convict in a barrel with a monkey, a rooster, a dog, and a venomous snake and rolling the barrel into the sea.

20. Vargas Machuca seems to be referring to an attack on a Pijao village related in *The Indian Militia*, 172–73.

sentiment, "Well, if you wish to keep me from this, why did you not keep those dogs from eating my father, mother, siblings, wife, and children, as I was the only one of the family who escaped? And if we are Christians, why do you not protect us from these savages?" Tears fell from his eyes as he said this, and knowing that what he said with tears and reason was true, I was moved to pity in such a manner that I returned his swords and left him, and continued moving through the battle. Later, a soldier who was with me at the time told me, "It is very wise to be permissive with your friends and severe with your enemies, for if you were to prevent their vengeance, they would turn their arms against us, and if they went away and left us alone we would be lost, for they would have already called for help and it would be near. What we saw should cause no surprise, for if we look back, we will see that Tain, the cacique, and his people are making meat [out of the enemy]." And I turned and saw more than fifty friendly [allied] Indians with heads and others with pieces of the enemies put on a wheel, singing their victory, and though I wished to prevent them from taking such vengeance, it was impossible. I felt pity upon seeing this, but I was forced to ignore it. And as I began gathering my Spanish soldiers, I turned my attention to a *caney* or *buhío* [thatch-roofed dwelling] where the captives who had not yet been eaten were, who had taken notice [i.e., of what was occurring] and had gathered themselves together against the danger presented to them by both Indian and Spaniard in the fighting. Several unarmed men went forward on my behalf, some using stones and others with weapons they found on the way, and each one crying out that they were Christians; I took the people I found to the square, where I could protect them without their kneeling at my feet. At this time, the enemy was entering the village to come to their aid, but they saw that all was lost, and that the Spaniards and the Indian allies were in order and gathering the people together; the enemy thus began to retreat and I sent out a squadron of Spaniards and Indian allies after them, whereupon they fled.

These captives told me of many cruelties done by a people given to such butchery that if the Bishop of Chiapa were to hear them it would seem to him that they were given quite extraordinary punishment. Some were at hand, including the cacique who had confessed to the crime he was convicted of, and justice was given; he was hanged within two hours and no memory remained of him. By

way of celebrating their triumph, the Indian allies took him away
in pieces, and I believe that to this day each one keeps what he took.
And returning to the captives, I say that in two months they had
eaten seventy of the hundred people, and had I waited longer, none
would have remained. The Indians in that land [the Pijaos of New
Granada's upper Magdalena Basin] are a people so fierce and savage that there is a public slaughterhouse for human flesh, and to
sustain it they have depopulated the entire valley of Neiva, whose
length runs sixty leagues, eating all the people inhabiting it. It has
been verified that in the past, and even when the Spaniards entered,
there were 200,000 Indians there; more than 100,000 have been eaten
and publicly weighed. Our [soldiers] have not been able to prevent
this, though they have always tried with weapons in hand, and more
than 1,000 Spaniards have died in the attempt. And returning to my
purpose, as I was unable to stop the friendly Indians from bloodying
themselves so with their enemies, the same will surely have occurred
to many other commanders; so that the Bishop attributes the cruelties to none other than the Spaniard, without taking proper account
and distinction of the matter, when he should grant the Spaniard the
punishment and the Indian the cruelty and vengeance, as it is quite
natural for them to seek out vengeance and cause death where there
has been death, for this is a part of them throughout their entire
lives, eating and killing one another.

In response to what the Bishop claims regarding our soldiers
burning many Indians alive and bringing dogs raised on human flesh
to tear them apart, I will briefly mention but two examples, and the
reasons for bringing dogs I will leave for later. As to burning them,
it so happened that a commander and a small number of soldiers had
gone in search of a group of marauding Indians, called the Carares, because of the great many robberies and deaths that they had
caused Spanish soldiers and the friars that accompanied them on the
great Magdalena River, which runs more than 250 leagues from its
source in the New Kingdom of Granada to Cartagena, on the coast,
bringing water to its lands and villages.[21] They chanced upon them
one day, unnoticed, finding them in drunken council in two large
thatched huts separated by a square. The soldiers took the square and

21. Vargas Machuca is here referring to himself in the third person. For more on
this incident, see *The Indian Militia*, xlvii–li.

surrounded the huts, but the Indians resisted and fought valorously from behind embrasures; and as the Indians saw well through the embrasures and most shot with their bows and arrows, the [soldiers] aiming at them could not see them and were unable to cause damage, and most of them received wounds with a grave and deadly poison. The commander, seeing the damage they were causing and the little effect of his soldiers and harquebuses, and [knowing] that if they took too long in defeating them they would all perish, as the aid from surrounding enemy villages was soon expected if one Indian were to escape or if the harquebus reports were heard, decided, after conferring with his [men], to set fire to them, and it was a wise resolution, for if they had not done it, none of his soldiers would have escaped; it was victory or death, finding themselves fifty leagues from help from any Christian settlements and receiving heavy damage, expecting enemy reinforcements to arrive at any moment. Setting [the huts] on fire was done with the intention of forcing them to surrender or come out into the open to fight as equals, each man for himself. The commander himself, with much risk to his own person, approached and lit the fire and the Indians were so pertinacious that, though a few came out, the others were burnt inside with no desire to come out and fight nor surrender. Here, what blame can be given to the Spaniards if their intention was none other than to force them out and save their lives, making use of this method, allowable in such a difficult case, where they would have doubtlessly lost them [i.e., their lives] had fire not been set? And I believe the Bishop of Chiapa would have naturally done the same if he did not wish to die a martyr; and so it seemed to the friar to whom the aforementioned commander confessed, that he would have done the same to save his life and the others as well if the company and people were his responsibility. In the Indies, many similar cases have occurred in this way, [appearing as] cruelties when simply told, yet free from this name when the circumstances of the occurrence are explained.

On this same occasion and conflict, it so happened to this same commander, having captured Indian men and women, bringing them with him as he traveled through the land in peace, [and calling upon] the caciques to surrender their criminals for punishment and to bring them to peace and service, that the whole land gathered together to attack the Spaniards and finish them off and, those [Indians] who were accustomed to the practice, to eat them. This happened to another commander and his company a few years before this, having entered the land to punish [the guilty]. One night the sentinels dropped their guard and all were killed, perishing at the hands of the Indians who planned on doing the same to the commander and his company, pursuing them so much with ambushes and skirmishes that they found themselves in great peril. It happened that one night they were surrounded, and the commander, seeing that they were in a bad position and in much danger, prepared and reinforced [his camp] as best he could. In a short while, they began to hear the murmurings of the enemy all around them, approaching little by little, and they were powerless. It so happened that among the Indian men and women of that land that they had brought with them for the aforementioned purpose, there were six or seven who had children at their breasts and who, sensing their own people so close by and wanting to do something to free themselves, began to pinch their children. Feeling the pain from the pinches, they raised such a clamor and cried so much that the sentinels and guards at their posts were unable to hear anything, saying that "the enemy is coming but we cannot hear them unless that racket is silenced." With such a disturbance, the commander did not know what course to take, for if he beat the women so that they silenced their children, the noise of their crying and pleas would be so great that the [approaching] Indians would know where they were. It is said that the best wedge is made from the same wood, and the best patch from the same cloth, so finally, on the sound advice of an Indian cacique, an ally and Christian, and according to what had occurred in similar situations during conquest or punishment (and as we have said, council in wartime should be received only from a man of experience), the Indian said these words, "Captain, why do you not give an order to take a child from one of these women and drown it in that river? You will see how the others will silence their own, afraid that the same will happen to them, and by silencing this disturbance, we will be able to defend ourselves though we are in a bad position." Forced by the danger that was so close and in order to save his people, the commander ordered that this be executed in the manner proposed by the cacique and, after first baptizing it [the infant], the deed was done. With this, all the noise was silenced, and though the enemy was seen here and there, he had to retreat, for he recognized the preparedness and defense of the Spaniards; this act was done in order to escape from that land, taking much advantage of the

Indians and the punishments, so that the robberies and murders done by the attackers ceased for some time. This commander recounted the deed with a theologian, and was absolved by his confession, and in the conversation they had afterward, he told him and made him understand that it is permitted to take one life in order to prevent so many deaths, as well as the damage that would result by not having done this, which, one fears, would be contrary to charity if such scandals were rewarded with peace, for it is better that one should perish than all humanity. If this deed were told and recounted alone, anyone would condemn it as being iniquitous and evil, but if the Bishop of Chiapa were to understand the reason behind all that he wrote so blatantly, he too would have given absolution, and all who read of it would have done the same.

With regard to his claims that the conquerors were given to training dogs in order to tear apart the Indians, it can also be said that they tolerated the use of harquebuses to kill them, a more certain death than with dogs. However, just as the harquebus has its purpose in frightening, offending, and defending, so does the use of dogs, for they are useful in the wars in those lands, and many provinces have been pacified in less time and at the cost of fewer lives, both of our own as well as theirs, by the way we use them. As he is a pious cleric rather than a soldier, the Bishop ignored this [parallel]: that if I am permitted to use the harquebus in peace and in war, why am I not permitted to use a dog as long as I do not misuse him? And may the one who should stray from that which is honestly permitted be punished; for that is why there is God, king, and justice. Dogs are used in mountainous lands, as they are not at all useful in open land free of forest and undergrowth, where other tactics are used. They are brought to save us from many dangers: they discover the ambushes that the Indians often prepare in wooded lands (for by their discovery, they cannot harm the people) and guard the camp, sensing the Indians from afar by the odor of their body paint made of pigment and turpentine, with which the warrior paints his face and body in order to appear more fierce. Once the people are noticed, the dog runs after them, barking, and the Indians stop, for they greatly fear them, and at the same time our [soldiers] ready their arms and are alerted; and until dogs were used, we were defeated many times because they came upon us unnoticed at night, which in those parts is much darker than the night is in Spain, as the sphere [of the sun] is directly [overhead] and there is no twilight from the sun such as when it is at an oblique [angle], which is why in Spain the sun has not quite set when night falls, but rather there is daylight for an hour afterwards. If the night itself is so dark there, forested lands are even more obscure when there is no moon, for the moon there is brighter than in these parts [i.e., in Spain] since its light falls directly. So with such darkness in the forests, and the Indians being naked and stepping so subtly that when they wish to make an assault they all come dragging their bellies on the ground like serpents, and the phlegmatic nature they are gifted with, there is a great need on our part of armed preparedness, as has been stated. In ambushes, dogs are greatly advantageous in pursuing a fleeing Indian, and there are many benefits in catching him, so that the lands do not rebel in case he is a spy or escaped prisoner; in this manner, success in our endeavors is secured. They are also useful during a conflict or skirmish, to detain the people who flee and to capture some who, if they are Indian headmen or caciques, are cause enough to pacify the land. And I will not deny that at times these Indians are bitten by the dogs but, as the Indian does not defend himself but rather prostrates himself, they are trained to do nothing more than bark until the soldier arrives, who always follows behind to take the captive and keep the dog from doing harm. Many new towns and estates have been defended with dogs, keeping the Indians from burning them because of the fear they have of the dogs, who sense and smell them and go out to the path and keep them away. Many captives (both Spaniard and Christian Indians) and stolen horses have been taken back from the Indians by using dogs, though they may have been taken two or three leagues into the forests, and it would not be exaggerating if one said six or eight [leagues]. The dogs are released where the enemy begins his retreat, following the trail so diligently that they come upon the prisoner; and if he has by chance crossed some large river, it is marvelous to see what the dogs do at the river banks, lacking only speech. Finally, depending on the river, the soldiers either make a bridge, or rafts, or take the dogs across by swimming or finding a sandbar, and once across, they are back on the trail. The Spaniards and conquerors are aided by dogs for these and other advantageous purposes; and that which is necessary may be called a just war; and the use of dogs is justified because of the aforementioned reasons, not to commit cruelties. The Christians gain nothing from this, nor

pursue it, nor is this their intention, but rather extending the faith
of Christ and to use the land. And if there are no Indians, neither
one of these things can be accomplished, and so it is advantageous
and necessary to conserve those they find and discover. But above all
other things, sustaining the lives of the settlers is to be expected, and
self defense is permitted even in newly conquered lands, for if the
Indians attempt to kill the Spaniards and begin to take such action, it
is not of great importance if [the Spaniards] kill them in defending
themselves. And among those who have given peace and obedience
and have received the Holy Gospel and baptism, if they should revolt
and burn the churches and kill the Spanish inhabitants or some part
of them, the punishment is licit and quite just. As Erasmus says [in
Education of a Christian Prince], "Punishment is just for those who,
of their will, offend and cause harm."

There are three types of Indians one should consider here. [First,
there are] some who have no knowledge of the Spaniards, but the
Spaniards know of them and that they are good and numerous people, and the land is fertile and abundant, and for these reasons, worthy of conquest. These people are approached with all the gentleness
in the world, with peace at the fore and offering it with gifts that are
sent to them. And most of these Indians and provinces, either those
needing the favor of the Spaniards against their enemies, or those
who are good by nature and are inclined to unbreakable friendship, as
we will later speak of, are treated kindly and are given much affection and benefit. And if they are a people who wish to fight and not
receive the Holy Gospel nor friendship, they do nothing but defend
themselves here, and because of this it is necessary to face them with
arms in hand; and by doing this and offering peace at the same time,
they come to receive and keep peace.

There is another kind of Indians whom the Spaniards, though
they know of them, do not seek out, as they are but few and their
lands are poor, such that any people who should settle there would be
unable to maintain themselves. They are savages with evil inclinations, who eat human flesh. These attack [on the] roads and murder
and are neither sought out nor disturbed. [Indians] such as these
deserve the punishment that would judiciously be given to them, and
not only punishment, but enslavement as well.

The other kind of Indians are those who, after having cunningly
accepted peace and obedience, and having received the Holy Gospel

and baptism, revolt with great destruction and cruelties that they
do to the Spaniards they lay their hands on, as has been said, burning churches and towns; and later they flee to the hills and forests
where they perish for the aforementioned reasons. All or most of the
Indians of the isles of Hispaniola, Cuba, and San Juan in Puerto Rico,
and Trinidad and others nearby have been of this type, some of whom
are savage Indians who travel the coasts of Tierra Firme and the isles
with their great canoes [*piraguas*], robbing and killing Christian
Indians as well as Spaniards, and [attacking] the fleets arriving from
Tierra Firme and New Spain that often stop there for water, such as
on La Deseada [Basse-Terre, Guadeloupe] and Dominica, Matalino
[Martinique], and others, where it has happened that they cause
much harm to the people who step ashore. They have been seen to
come upon ships, alone and at anchor on the coasts of these and other
islands, boarding by night and finding the people sleeping, whereupon they cut the throats of everyone and eat them and sink the
ships after first looting them and capturing men and women, and to
this day they make use of those who escaped death.[22] These are the
ones whom the Bishop, in his treatise, says the Spaniards make slaves
of, and certain of my vote, this should not be prevented but rather
permitted, so as to finally be rid of such evil and savage people who
cause so much harm. The Chichimecs in New Spain were sentenced
to ten years of slavery by a council of great theologians, as were the
Pijaos in the New Kingdom of Granada and in the East Indies [i.e.,
the *moros* on Mindanao, Philippines]; in some places it was quite
just [to enslave] these pernicious and dangerous savages, though the
former [i.e., Chichimecs] are especially so, the latter are not. The Chichimecs of New Spain, as we will later show, are now pacified, weary
of being pressured so.

And returning to the isle of Hispaniola to conclude, although I
have already stated [that] the cause of their [i.e., the native Taínos']
complete deterioration is not because of the reasons the Bishop
offers; but in order to ponder and exaggerate this, he claims that
there were five powerful kings with no other innumerable lesser
lords, and that these also were destroyed. May it here be known
that they were not kings, but caciques, and the other lords were his

---

22. For examples of these kinds of Carib attacks in Vargas Machuca's day, see Peter
Hulme and Neil Whitehead, eds., *Wild Majesty: Encounters with Caribs from Columbus to the Present Day* (New York: Oxford University Press, 1992), 38–79.

captains, with factions, relatives, and governors from other towns, and it is humorous to call them kings when in those parts only two could be legitimately named thus: Monteçuma [Moctezuma II] in New Spain and Atabalipa [Atawallpa] in Peru, so powerful and with royal spirit in their dealings, wealth, and governance. The rest are laughable, for if all the caciques were called kings, I think there were and are more than 50,000 of them in the Western Indies, and this is neither exaggeration nor hyperbole, and if they all deserved to be called kings, one could easily say that my soldiers and I had subjected and conquered more than 500. The truth be told, these caciques are savages. If it is a hot land, they are naked and sleep on the ground, in beds, or in hanging *hamacas,* and their food is wretched. They lay their food on straw that they place on the ground, and serve it in *totumas* or *mates* that they make from gourds, without any tablecloths. The queens are as naked as the kings, and if there is any difference between these and the rest of the people, it is that they are more bellicose and brave, for succession is extraordinarily guarded, and among them there is nothing but tyranny; and if the true successor were to follow, it was only by being bellicose.[23] There were caciques among these who subjected 20,000 Indians, and others, 10,000, or 4,000 or 2,000, and others but 100 or even 10, and if one said less, it would hardly be lying as it is all true. But he who led 10,000 had no more authority than he who led 100; such is their manner of kings. I confess that the five mentioned by the Bishop must have had more than 10,000, but not one of them could get more than 4,000 combatants to the battlefield, and anyone who could, would have been quite powerful. This applies to the isle of Santo Domingo [Hispaniola] and in torrid lands, in the islands as well as on Tierra Firme, because in cold lands the people are clothed and the caciques are more powerful, and the two who deserved the title of kings, as mentioned, ruled over a great many vassals. But in the rest of the islands and torrid lands, it is as I have said. Take note of who is given the title of king, as they only say this because of the punishments done to them.

While taking some caciques to Spain, God allowed Spaniards to drown along with them inside the ships, and one should first believe that it was divine will that such idolatrous and perverse people should not escape, and that he wished to establish his Holy Faith in

---

23. Vargas Machuca shifts to past tense here.

that land, populating it with Christian and Spanish people. This is also easily seen in the steps Christopher Columbus took in discovering the Indies, making use of a Portuguese pilot returning to Spain from East India, who suffered a storm so great and ceaseless that he came upon the isle of Santo Domingo. At the time he discovered this all the people on the ship were sleeping, and he marked the land with his compass, as well as the latitude, and ordered the sails to be turned to take another course so that none but himself could see it or speak of it. And so it was, keeping his secret, that this pilot came to die in the house of Columbus, to whom he revealed [his secret].[24] And taking this story, [Columbus] studied it, and therefore went to Portugal and France, and none of the kings gave him credit, and ultimately God placed him in the hearts of the Catholic sovereigns, Ferdinand and Isabella, of glorious memory, so that they prepared ships for his journey. Who would have thought that storms are fought on the sea as they are among people, arriving to such straits that one may be thrown into the sea today, left until the morning perhaps, or maybe the afternoon, being taken for a swindler or a charlatan?

God delayed this discovery hour by hour until he placed the land in their [i.e., Ferdinand and Isabella's] hands with a safe and peaceful harbor; and this demonstrates that it was divine will arranging each event with such strange means, for if it were any other, such as those who were present at the time, whether it was Columbus on the sea or the other conquerors who accompanied him, if He wished to prevent anything that occurred along their journey, He would have; and the caciques would not have died nor any of the other Indians. I maintain, without being a theologian, that no leaf falls from the tree but by divine will, and that, as St. Paul says, for those who love God, everything is converted into good; and if it is true that God favors the Spaniards in those parts [the Indies] and disfavors the idolatrous Indians, some are guarded and some are destroyed miserably. Truth is the daughter of time, which reveals all things.

24. The "anonymous pilot" legend was first published by Fernández de Oviedo in 1535, where Vargas Machuca likely picked it up. See Nicolás Wey Gómez, *Tropics of Empire: Why Columbus Sailed South to the Indies* (Cambridge, Mass.: MIT Press, 2008), 45.

After the most exceedingly great and abominable tyrannies that these men
committed in the city of Mexico and in the cities and much land around (ten
and fifteen and twenty leagues from Mexico, in which an infinite number of
people were slain), he [Cortés] passed his tyrannical plague and pestilence
farther on, and it did spread into and defile and lay waste to the province of
Pánuco, which was a wondrous thing, the multitude of people that the prov-
ince had and the devastations and slaughters that he wrought there.
                                                    —*Fray Bartolomé de las Casas*

The Second Discourse and Defense
Rebuttal and justification of the conquests of
the Kingdom of New Spain.

If it is true, as common sense dictates, that one is prohibited from
being both accuser and sentencing judge in the same legal matter,
as is the Bishop, [then] he infringes upon this just precept by using
these two powers, accusing, collectively, all the conquerors and settlers who have been and are in the Western Indies and Windward and
Leeward isles, without exception, and who have been, as I have stated,
so numerous [even] without the five generals (as has been said and
will be addressed again in its time and place), and at the same time, as
a judge, [he] sentences all of them, with no exceptions, to perpetual
hell. This power competes with [that of] the one God who knows who
is condemned to hell and who is predestined; and He is a fair judge
who makes the charge and accepts the justification [for it], who uses
justice along with his divine mercy, so that because of it, though they
may have been evil, perverse, and iniquitous, all the conquerors may
hope for salvation.

And returning to our purpose, I state that in his treatise, the
Bishop pursues the valorous don Hernando Cortés and his companions through New Spain, which they entered in 1518, and he
addresses this [event] in as confusing and general [terms] as he has
with others, changing the names of the landforms and coasts, as
can be seen in his book, as well as the distances, villages, number
of peoples, events, and cruelties with which he says the Spaniards
ruined and destroyed this whole kingdom, as well as 2,000 leagues of
the province of Tierra Firme. Well, we know for a fact and evidence
shows us that the Spaniards never trod upon more than 70 leagues of
its length, from the limits of [the Gulf of] Urabá in the east, [whose]

Indians were never conquered, to Veragua in the west. Some are between Cartagena and Nombre de Dios and others between the province of Tierra Firme and Veragua. And if we count the province of Veragua, we could add an additional 50 leagues, for a total of 120 (Tierra Firme cannot be counted, as it is subordinate to the Royal Audiencia of Panama). Subtracting 120 from 2,000, the land remaining is 1,880 [leagues long]. The distance from north to south [i.e., the width of Panama] measures 18 to 20 leagues at its narrowest, which is from Portobelo to Panama [City], and from the Northern Sea to the Southern, at the widest point, it measures no more than 30, full of mountains and forests. And if there are any dwellings, there are but few, as the short distance of the land has shown there are few Indians who can live there; those who do are similar to those on the isle of Santo Domingo, as the disposition of the land is similar or even worse, being of such poor and infertile quality and lower altitude. Everyone knows that Tierra Firme is this narrow, and if not, we will prove it, as there are mountain peaks in the middle of this land that can be seen from both seas, which is the reason it is called Tierra Firme, as its first discoverers were to observe both seas from its heights, thinking that there would be a strait of water passing from one sea to the other, but they found that this was not so and that the land continued, and so they called it Tierra Firme.

And returning to the cruelties of which he accuses these discoverers, I say that his manner of writing and the great scandal that he has caused (and will continue to cause) place differing and varying thoughts in human understanding and that, as St. Bernard says (*De precep e disciplin*),[25] one scandal is poorly redressed with another; such that if any cruelty was done by one particular person, as is possible, it seems to me that such a general and overbearing accusation that would scandalize everyone was not just, and I believe he would take up arms against any enemy who should offend the honor of his homeland in any way. Seeing my evidence and justification, each [person] will think according to what his judgment dictates.

One may well understand how God prepared, ordered, and guided the entry of don Hernando Cortés into New Spain, and by the events and results one may judge the principles and means, because as Titus

25. Vargas Machuca's marginal reference, "*De precep e disciplin*," is likely a reference to St. Bernard's *Praecepto et dispensatione*.

Livy says, the outcome of things is the teacher of the ignorant. We may examine, then, the beginning of this entrance and who did it, his virtue and customs, in what manner God favored it and the results it had. On the nineteenth of November in the year 1518, don Hernando Cortés left from Santiago de Cuba with his fleet to reconnoiter New Spain. He arrived with good weather [and suffered] neither disasters nor impediment. God willing, he first came upon a land called Coçumil [Cozumel], whereupon a cacique named Calahuni came out to give an agreeable welcome, as the story goes, and behind him a Spaniard named Aguilar, who had become lost on that coast many years before, along with others, now dead. This [Aguilar] was comfortable living with the Indians and served as an interpreter along with his wife, Marina. When [Cortés] took on these two interpreters in such a strange situation, he had them married by a cleric in order to better facilitate his purpose, as it was the work of God, and Hernando Cortés himself was the sponsor.[26] Aided by the interpreters, he explored the coast, pointing the prow [of his ship] toward San Juan de Ulúa and the river of Veracruz, the port nearest the city of Mexico, as if he knew or had seen the description of the land on some chart, course [description], or map. He landed ashore and, being well received by the Indians, God gave him the idea to sink the ships. This act and decision came from heaven, for I doubt that a human could have done so; he knew not where he was, nor what could befall him, nor what they might need; and as Democritus says, if accompanied by discretion and wisdom, such daring is of great advantage. Where Monteçuma [Moctezuma II], the highest lord of that place, resided was known in Mexico and [Cortés] went to seek him; on the road, God gave him those who would favor and guide him in discovering the land and in sustaining his army, such as in the war that they later began to fight. He found himself favored by an entire province of Indians, the best in those parts with regards to their condition, respectful, courteous, and brave; they are called Tascaltecs [Tlax-calteca, or Tlaxcalans] and the province is Tascala [Tlaxcala], with whom peace and friendship lasted and will last for many years to come. They later received our Holy Catholic faith better than any

26.   Vargas Machuca is here compressing and confusing the stories of Spanish cast-away Jerónimo de Aguilar, picked up by Cortés in February 1519 on the coast of Yucatan, and doña Marina, or Malintzin, taken shortly afterward in Tabasco. They were never married.

others, as well as good government and noble comportment, for they are noble and from the first day were accepted as such, enjoying such privilege and good graces by royal concession; and they, as well as the Spaniards, are in such agreement, that there is no Indian who would injure nor dislike a Spaniard, nor any Spaniard who would offend them. This happens to such an extent that, in the city of Mexico or along a road, if a Spaniard asks an unknown Indian for some service and the Indian tells him, "Lord, I am a nobleman, I am Tascaltec," the Spaniard not only leaves him alone, but also shows him respect with particular pleasure, and I have seen this happen many times and it has happened to me. Here, we may observe those words of Quintilian, that virtue is the inheritance of the successors; and Marcus Aurelius says that virtue makes the stranger a native, and the native a stranger to vice, which these Tascaltecs demonstrate well, for they are less given to vice than any other Indians, and we treat them as equals, and we accept them as natives with noble correspondence; they deserve to be received well because of the great faith they have maintained without corruption, and the help that this [faith] has given us.

As St. Augustine says (*De fide rerum invisibilium*), true friendship is the bond and the link between all things, and good works are the fetters of noble hearts. The opinion of the Bishop of Chiapa is based on these [Indians], and he publishes his treatise of these virtues for all the Indians, from which we are able to see [him] as having some reason. With these Indians of so laudable and noble a condition, neither the Bishop nor we may ever allege cruelties or punishments. In the end, don Hernando Cortés entered and kept Mexico with their help; had God not provided him with such good people, there is no doubt that he would have lost. Because of this we know that in his engagements and battles, finding himself with so few Spaniards and Tascaltecs compared to so many enemies, God wished for him to be favored many times over by St. Peter and St. James, the patron of Spain, and this was clear to both sides. Later, to reinforce victory and stability, Pánfilo de Narváez found himself in dire need, as his story recounts, with a good number of Spaniards and no hope of rescue, nor understanding of the reason for their arrival, which was extraordinary; and he was able to subject [the Indians] to his governance. We must consider that this was ordained by God, that his divine will desired that Holy Faith to be taken to those regions, for their great Christianity [i.e., that of the Spaniards] must have deserved it [i.e.,

this honor]. After this, all the remaining provinces of New Spain
were conquered in such a brief time by the Marquis del Valle,
preserving [Cortés's] succession with such great fame and renown in
his service and that of the King, our lord.[27] This great gentleman and
Christian, why should he deserve the title of cruel tyrant? His works
and deeds were so courtly that they corresponded to his lineage,
treating religion with such respect and teaching the Indians in such a
way that may times it was observed that, when he came upon a
priest, he would get off of his horse and kiss his hand with a knee on
the ground, and [the Indians] would do the same, learning such fine
behavior that they, remembering their teacher, have always done this
to such an extent that the old Indians weep for him. And St. Augustine says (*ser. 48 de temp*) that the spirit of man is inclined toward
God or the Devil; and one believes that the spirit of the good marquis
would be directed toward God and that he would do nothing that was
not in his service. And if the Bishop understood the strategies of war
and its principles, I believe he would be convinced that, as Vegetius
says (*De re militari*), "In war, opportunity generally proves more
helpful than virtue and strength."[28] As the marquis was responsible
for guarding and keeping his army, it was necessary for him to
prepare not only for the present, but for that which was to come as
well, for if he had not done this he would not deserve the title of good
commander and governor. As an example, warning would arrive from
his spies, either Spanish or friendly Indians, that [other Indians] were
in council preparing to attack him and his people; he verified this and
once satisfied, he attacked before their forces were gathered, and as an
astute captain, defeated them. This deed would not be untimely nor
without purpose, but rather the preparation of good governance. As
Cicero says (*Pro numera*), he who governs must not only attend to
what he does, but also to what is to come; and to avoid great harm,
one must act according to principles, for if they are not observed, the
one who should forget to show severity in war and clemency in
peace, punishing evil and rewarding goodness, will lose; as

27. Cortés's succession was hardly as secure as Vargas Machuca claims. The mar-
quisate, granted by Charles V in 1529, was suspended in 1567 following the rebellion of
Martín Cortés. Its territories were divided in 1574 and the title only partially restored in
1594.

28. The reference is to early fifth-century writer Publius Flavius Vegetius Renatus,
author of *De re militari*.

Democritus says, the world is governed by two things: reward and punishment.[29] The Tascaltecs are rewarded for their virtue and faith; and those who have given peace and received faith but have broken this with extortions and murders are punished. Here Livy warns (*Lib 8. dec. 1*) that not punishing at the proper time leads to much harm and evil, for by neglecting to do this, the [person] to be punished defends himself, trying to kill the punisher, and all the rest behind him, making it necessary to use arms.[30] And because of what we have said, we have done our duty and satisfied our obligations to all the provinces of this kingdom, there being but one language,[31] continuing later to Peru, where I will reward the great number of Indians who were and are in New Spain, as well as those few who, as the Bishop says, have been left with a division and account so certain and clear that everyone may be satisfied.

After the Indians were calmed and no longer wished to try their arms against us, both Spaniards and Tascaltecs, the land was distributed, giving the town divisions and *encomiendas* to each Spanish soldier for two generations, as their majesties the monarchs [Ferdinand and Isabella] and Emperor Charles V had ordered, according to the merit and quality of each [soldier]. And in order to sustain our [people], each assigned Indian was ordered to deliver a certain quantity [of goods] to his encomendero and administrator each year, according to the rate decided upon, obligating the encomendero, at his own cost, to teach the [Christian] doctrine to them and address their complaints, cure their illnesses, recover fugitives, and other [responsibilities] of greater or lesser importance. There is a greater multitude and the land is full of a greater number of these Indians now than at earlier times, because the Spanish encomendero in the beginning had but a fourth of the income for each year from only the tribute that the Indian was obligated to pay. This same income has the same tax rate, without alteration, and according to this, there are many people. I would like to demonstrate that there are a great many more. Count the *mestizos*

29. The writings of Democritus (ca. 460–370 B.C.E.) were mostly lost, but his views on reward and punishment appeared in Plutarch and other writers frequently read in Spanish translation in Vargas Machuca's time. It is likely Vargas Machuca also got his knowledge of Cicero on clemency and severity from Plutarch's *Lives,* although collections of his speeches were also widely available in Spanish.

30. The reference is apparently to book 2 of Livy's *History of Rome.*

31. Here and at the opening of the next defense, Vargas Machuca seems to assume that all conquered Mexicans were Nahuatl speakers.

or *montañeses*, which they call the children of Spaniards and Indians, and there is a great number; and also of those *çambahigo* [i.e., *zambos*], who are children of blacks and Indians, there are many also and they fill the land; and likewise the great many Spanish-speaking Indians and domestic servants [*yanaconas*] who work in the cities of the Spaniards, who cannot be counted as part of those who pay tribute who so fill the land, both males and females, and who are a great many. Take into account so many officials who live in the cities and who are innumerable in the entire kingdom, but who also cannot be counted among those who pay tribute, but who also occupy the land; and likewise consider the number of Indians who wander outside of their towns of origin, employed in strange lands, on farms with livestock, in sugar mills, mines and other greater or lesser estates, and on military expeditions, who also multiply the number and increase in the land, and the caciques forget about them. In paying tribute, it is likely that the caciques hide many Indians, so that the encomendero does not know if they are dead or alive or if he has ever known of them, for the caciques reserve these in order to have them for some particular tribute and service, and these also populate the land. These calculations are always averaged, and when one part is lacking, another part provides, regardless of those who might die of overwork, which almost never occurs in cold and temperate lands, except [those who die] from the general illnesses that occasionally befall them, such as typhus, pleurisy, pox, and bloody diarrheas [dysentery] that often sweep away a great number of them, and these are so common that there is no place that escapes them. Only Spaniards native to Spain are free from these illnesses, and even in this, God wishes to show that He is better served with these places populated by Spaniards than by the natives themselves, for it happened that a million Indians in all three kingdoms died of a common illness, but not even fifty Spaniards died of it; and if these illnesses did not happen so often, their multiplying would be so great that [the Indians] would not fit into all the Indies. With all of this, and the great number [of Indians], the calculation I have given remains standing and would still even if an [illness] so great were to come and finish them all, for then it would be known to be entirely the will of God that none of them remain. And I state that in hot lands this number does not apply, but rather what I said when addressing the isle of Santo Domingo and the coasts; and it will be understood that the Indians do not simply die from work, as the Bishop says, but rather there are many benefits and advantages for them, as has been said, for as St. Basil says, idleness is the beginning of evil deeds; and as St. Chrysostom says (*Sup. 6 en hom. 14*), it teaches and shows all evil. The Indians carry heavy burdens on their shoulders and remove their clothing for the purpose, an old custom of theirs, and at times they offer themselves in order to earn their pay, and so that their horses may rest in the fields, the Indians carry the loads themselves; and they do not do this because they love to work, but rather to keep their horses from working, placing more value on the horses than on themselves. And I confess that sometimes they are compelled to carry loads for pay and they do so quite contentedly, not only in their own interest, but also because they are accustomed to this ever since the world was created, just as day-laborers in Spain and other places shoulder loads and do other, more difficult labor. The Indians can also be seen doing the following, however: having received their pay, they drop their burdens in the middle of the road and far from town, as if they were attending to their necessities, and run off. And if a Spaniard is going along with them, he is able neither to go ahead nor to turn back until finally, hunger gets the best of him and he is forced to hide the load and reach the closest town to find help to carry it; and more often than not the load is lost, as mentioned, because of entrusting it to the Indians. And if it is wine, they know very well how to break the cask and drink it, and once they are drunk, they do not return for a month or two.

These Indians from New Spain are the best governed in all the Indies, which can well be seen in all their occupations and arts that they pursue and learn with such perfection; in the end they are more clever than others, which is why they have persevered in Christian consideration, being diligent in serving the divine cult, adorning the temples well,[32] and providing them all with music, and [providing] the churches and monasteries with great, illustrious buildings; and their lay brotherhoods show great courtesy, care, and preparation for the processions with many artful dances. I dare say that on a day during Corpus Christi, in the city of Mexico, [the procession] is so solemn and distinguished that such a concentration of Christianity has no equal, and that, without exaggeration, the Indians perform more

---

32. The Royal Palace transcription states that the Indians have great *fervor* in the temples (*ardor* instead of *adorno; CDI,* 262).

than two hundred dances, each with its own standard, and if [the celebration] has diminished since then, in my time [ca. 1578] it occurred as I have described. I saw our Holy Faith so well established there that I am certain that it will have grown; there is no more idol worshiping or sacrifices such as there once were, in this kingdom more than the others referred to, for there were so many victims sacrificed every day, as every historian who has studied this has affirmed, that never in all the world has anyone seen or heard of its equal.

It is argued how the good and holy religious teachers caused such a great change from one extreme to the other, and how, like a great gentleman and Christian, the leader [i.e., conquistador] would begin all of this; and as everyone knows, it was the Marquis del Valle, whose objective in his governing is easily seen, such that judging the means and the principle, we will find in him a great Christian name, virtuous, discreet, prudent, and charitable, faithful to his king, of elevated intellect, valorous and valiant, famous, fortunate, of great council and astute, merciful, magnanimous, diligent, meticulous in preparing for war and for peace, leaving the entire flowering kingdom so rich and abundant in all things, and [leaving] the Indians with knowledge of God, well-mannered in human life, shod, clothed, and fed, with more adornment in their houses and dwellings than they formerly had, horses to carry them and money to spend, possessions and farms like ours, the sciences of writing and reading, and especially that of music. In the end, there is nothing that the Spaniard accomplishes in which the Indian does not take part. In this way, nobility, estate, and contentment have come to the conquerors, and such wealth to our Spain, that she is the envy of foreign nations. To the successors of this great gentleman, estates [have been given], and upon their coats of arms a fame that will last forever. In the life to come, one may expect to have the same triumph and glory one had in this world. And if it seems I have exaggerated, look at his stories and make a wise judgment, and many more virtues will be found that I, with my limited understanding, have left unsaid, and I assure you that nothing but the truth has moved me, for I neither achieved what he did nor did I know him, and neither I nor my [people] ever received benefits from him, and I can say that I have never spoken to any of them. However, I believe that, because of this, he has no greater admirer in the world, for virtue, as Quintilian says, remains unto the last successors, and never ceases to be envied.

A few days afterward, the universal king and emperor of those kingdoms, who was called Atabalipa, came to where [Francisco Pizarro] was, and he came with many naked people and their laughable weapons, not knowing how swords cut and lances wounded, and how swiftly horses ran, and who the Spaniards were . . . and he came to the place where the Spaniards were, saying "Where are those Spaniards? Come out here. . . ." And the Spaniards came out to him and slew infinite numbers of his people, taking as their prisoner this king who had come on a litter; and when he was their prisoner, they treated for his ransom.

—Fray Bartolomé de las Casas

The Third Discourse and Defense
Rebuttal and justification of the conquests of
the Kingdom of Peru.

Therefore, as we have said in a general manner regarding New Spain, it being a tiresome thing to address the particulars, as the language and manner of conquests are the same, and also considering that as [things went] with the leader [Cortés] so it can be presumed [they went] with the other commanders he dispatched, we will here address that which applies only to the Kingdom of Peru, including all her provinces in one, excepting the Kingdom of Chile because more can be told [about it]; therefore, abbreviating as much as possible since the strongest evidence has already been given, and so as to not tire the reader, I state:

Peru was discovered and conquered by don Francisco Pizarro in the year 1535 [actually begun in 1532], and if the cruelties described by the Bishop [as being committed] in the Windward and Leeward isles and Hispaniola, as well as in Tierra Firme or New Spain, caused so much scandal, all the more so will those that he describes as taking place in the Kingdom of Peru, from that year up to 1552, which were truly incomparable. And because neither he nor I was present at that time, we are forced to keep up appearances with legitimate information and the strongest examples we can. Well, as a man who has traversed that kingdom and others in those lands [of South America] for more than thirty years, in peace as well as in war, I am able to legitimately offer my reason in the defense that I propose, and there may well have been some of the cruelties he mentions, but I am unable to defend these specifically. I will, however, speak in general, as the Bishop does, excluding no person among governors or conquerors, the whole of Peru having been depopulated of the natives because of them, where one must consider the same distribution, multiplication, and calculation as in New Spain, that though it is true that [in Peru] there is not such a great number of Indians as there [i.e., in New Spain], it is because there never were in their [time of] prosperity and past, but of those that were found in the beginning, the entire number of Indians remains, and if any have perished, they were but few, [and] it has been in the rebellions and conspiracies of the Spaniards with the concerns and labors that cause such altercations.[33] Because of this, they should not be attributed to cruelties, for at those times, generally, Spaniards perish as well as Indians. And to the intention of our defense, I will follow the entry that the Spaniards made into the lands of Peru, Pugna [Puná Island, near Guayaquil, Ecuador] being the first [place] they took, although the chroniclers who address this differ here regarding the discovery and the conquest of this island, for some say that the natives resisted our coming with great strength and war, and employed many great strategies, ruses, precautions, and betrayals, which obligated the general and soldiers to bloody their arms well until it was entirely pacified, from whence they passed to the mainland, six or eight leagues from there, to a port called Túmbes. The Bishop of Chiapa says [the natives] of this island welcomed our [people] with affection, giving them good service and lodging, providing all that was necessary, and that the pay they were given before [the Spaniards] left was to spear them and test the edges of their swords upon them, in such a manner that the island was left uninhabited and destroyed with unheard-of cruelties, and those who escaped with their lives were made slaves and taken away. In these different and easily found accounts such as that of the Bishop of Chiapa, printed in the year 1552, and that of Agustín de Zárate, printed in the year 1555, I adhere to that of the Bishop regarding the good welcome, treatment, and hospitality as being true.[34] I heard many accounts of this

33. The reference is to the so-called Peruvian Civil War, which began around 1540 as a blood feud between the Pizarro and Almagro families and led to Gonzalo Pizarro's rebellion against the crown, which ended in 1548.

34. Agustín de Zárate's *Historia del descubrimiento y conquista del Perú* was indeed published in Antwerp in 1555. Once translated, it fueled the Black Legend. See Maltby, *The Black Legend in England*, 21–23.

on the same island, as well as in Guayaquil, the closest city, where I made an investigation with care and curiosity; and with regards to the ill payment that our people gave them, it can only be denied as being quite contrary to fact and to what occurred. And if it were so, from such evil and thankless people no good thing can be expected; as St. Bernard says, ingratitude is an infernal deed and a cruel enemy of grace, for such kind hospitality as this, I confess, should not be repaid with anything but heroic and proper correspondence, demonstrating a noble spirit, virtuous and thankful, as good deeds are a common virtue in Peru. And on that same island I have heard, not once but many times, and as a guest and friend of the lord and cacique of it named don Francisco Tomalá, the story of the arrival of don Francisco Pizarro and his fleet, for he is the grandson of Tomalá, the cacique and native lord who received him [Pizarro] so well; and it is commonly said among the Indians and Spaniards of the nearby city of Guayaquil, farther up river, and some stories of Peru refer to it, saying that the fleet was well received, the general and soldiers receiving much affection and hospitality, each one receiving all possible gifts, according to the quality of his person. This is what I am able to say; and if it were true that part of the Indian [community] had any thoughts of harming our people, it must have been quickly resolved without as many deaths and destruction as the Bishop claims; and this is easily seen, and it is known that the punishment was light, and that the cacique and lord was not aware of it, nor was he present in the council gathered in order to kill Christians, as Agustín de Zárate writes in his history, that planned this and began to set it in motion.

The lord of this island was not only content to be a good host, but he and a great part of his people also joined in service to the royal standard [*Real*] like the Tascaltecs in New Spain, and guiding the Spanish fleet, they landed on Túmbes on the mainland, where they were met by armed Indians. And on this occasion, the cacique Tomalá was a great advantage to our people, and for the service, hospitality, and good deeds that the general received from him, he related this to His Majesty, who had grace upon him and his successors, giving them complete jurisdiction over the island, with no other justice but his, nor any encomendero nor administrator. And so it is for the cacique don Francisco Tomalá, as it has been for his ancestors and will be for his successors, by whose grace and concession the Indians pay tribute to him and to no other.[35] This cacique represents [true] lordly dignity, and so that his qualities be known, above all he is a great Christian, brave and gallant, always dressed in our courtly manner with shoes, cape, and hat, sword and gilded dagger on an embroidered sword-belt, a great musician of the *vihuela* [baroque guitar], and an expert dancer; he is a fine horseman and skilled in arms, courtly in our language and ceremonies, a great friend of Spaniards, such that if any Spanish ship should arrive at the island, and [there is] any gentle-man in service of the King within, he will find him and take him into his house as a guest and attend to him until his departure, and this hospitality is that of a lord, for he has a great palace with every room adorned with tapestries and taffeta draperies. He is served and obeyed by his vassals and domestic servants, and he married a Span-ish woman, a noble dame of fine appearance, who died after a few years, causing him great sadness. This cacique has great dockyards made for rigging ships, and I believe there are none other in the entire Southern Sea;[36] some of his people as well as Spaniards work there, brought as an agreement along that sea and coasts; the benefits received are from Spain, in return for what he did, and a close friend-ship has no less strength than family bonds. Here, each person may judge, according to his capacity, this discourse of the cruelties that the Spaniards did on this isle, considering the others in Peru about which the Bishop writes, according to the stories he chose, that if we had treated them well more often, we would have completely saved ourselves [from ill] appearances; however, regarding this, I believe what we address later will suffice.

The Spaniards arrived at Túmbes, along with the cacique Tomalá, as already mentioned, and once they defeated the Indians who confronted them with war and a great force of peoples from the surrounding areas who came to their aid, they settled and founded the city of San Miguel [de Piura] with these Indians.[37] And Francisco

35. Vargas Machuca is basically correct on the Tomalá family story. See Kris Lane, *Quito 1599: City and Colony in Transition* (Albuquerque: University of New Mexico Press), 89, 199, and Adam Szászdi, *Don Diego Tomalá, cacique de la Isla de la Puná: Un caso de aculturación socioeconómico* (Guayaquil: Museo del Banco Central, 1988).

36. The nearby shipyards of Guayaquil were the most important ones in the Span-ish Pacific at the time Vargas Machuca was writing, but others were located at Acapulco and Guatulco, Mexico, and at Cavite, near the Philippine capital of Manila.

37. Vargas Machuca is getting ahead of himself here, as it was directly after found-ing Piura that Pizarro and his 168 men set out for Cajamarca, where they captured the Inca Atawallpa in November 1532.

Pizarro found more than six hundred captive native men and women on the isle of Puná, and freed them from captivity along with one of his principal captains; and two days before the fleet left this island to return to Túmbes, he sent them to their cacique and lord with three Spanish soldiers, thinking that by this good deed he would find hospitality and deserved correspondence, but it was quite the contrary. At the moment the Spaniards reached Túmbes, the cacique and lord to whom they were guided, though quite happy and joyful to see his vassals liberated from captivity, sacrificed these three unfortunate Spaniards to his gods. Within three or four days Francisco Pizarro arrived with his fleet, and found himself in a such a predicament that it was an enormous labor and danger to go ashore and several soldiers were killed and wounded. But finally he took control of [the island] and aimed to exact a well-deserved punishment for the sacrifice of his soldiers. The cacique and lord of that province saw that many of his people were paying with their lives for something he was guilty of, so before [the Spaniards] were able to capture him, for they sought him diligently, he offered peace and obedience, and he was later received and pardoned of his crime and cruelty; I believe and am certain that [this would not have happened] in any other nation, and that his poor response deserved [punishment].

In this way, don Francisco Pizarro received news of Atabalipa [Atawallpa], king of part of Peru, or tyrant rather, because the true lord of those kingdoms by direct succession was his older brother Guascar Inga [Waskar Inka], who at the time resided in Cuzco. This Atabalipa not only rebelled with the province of Quito, but after taking control of it, he also returned with his army and conquered a great part of the kingdom, until he arrived at Caxamalca [Cajamarca], where he settled.[38] From there he sent his captains and part of his army to Cuzco, where his brother, the true king and lord, resided, and they were so bellicose, skilled, and valiant that they conquered and reduced to vassals of their lord Atabalipa all the provinces they passed through. Caciques and governors [were] given their positions by him, bringing a great number of people and combatants from

38. The Incas, like the Ottomans, practiced "unigeniture" rather than "direct succession," but Atawallpa and Guascar (now spelled Waskar), sons of Wayna Kapak, were indeed fighting for control of the empire when the Spanish arrived. Atawallpa did not "settle" at Cajamarca, but rather stopped to rest and visit its sacred hot springs. As with the conquest of Mexico, Vargas Machuca seems to be drawing from an eclectic mix of published chronicles and oral legends.

each province, such that once they arrived to where Guascar the king and his army were waiting for them, having received news of their coming, his army was ready for battle and so they were given it; and though the chroniclers differ on whether they were defeated in the first [battle] or the second, in the end, however it happened, he was captured by the captains of Atabalipa and his army was routed, and most of them either fled or were killed, and in this way the entire land was eventually surrendered [to Atabalipa]. And having settled everything in the name of Atabalipa Inga, they retreated and marched to Caxamalca, where they resided, taking the captive brother Guascar, [and they would have arrived] victoriously and joyfully if fortune had not crossed their path with such ill-fated news of the arrival of the Spaniards in the lands of Peru and so close to Caxa-malca, where they were forced to seek out their lord. This news was not so secret that the unfortunate King Guascar knew nothing about it, and though a prisoner and closely guarded, he was able to dis-patch his ambassadors to Túmbes, where the governor don Francisco Pizarro was, as we have said, settling the land. After welcoming him in their manner and language and making offers as if from a royal person, although captive, with much courtesy and pleasant words, the [ambassador] related the story of their origins and kingdom and how [Guascar] was the successor by direct male lineage, and the universal king of those kingdoms, because his father had conquered the land to the north [and had] died in Quito. His younger brother Atabalipa Inga stayed there, having traveled with [their father], and rebelled along with those provinces, declaring this and asking [Guascar] to accept it. But they were not inherited from their grandfather, but rather won by their father and neither of them had more right to them than the other. [Guascar] replied that [Atawallpa] should leave the lands as part of the royal crown, and that he would show him the provinces where he should live and maintain himself as a [royal] person and brother. Not satisfied with this promise, [Atawallpa] made war upon him in such a manner that he and his captains advanced, taking all the land, until utterly defeating him, capturing him, and taking him to Caxamalca where Atabalipa, his brother, resided. And since he was the true king and successor, he begged and insisted to be protected and aided, as he had the power to do so and had been well informed, and in return, he offered complete brotherhood and gener-ous recompense, and with this right, he could bloody his arms at will.

When these ambassadors arrived, the governor don Francisco Pizarro, leaving the city of San Miguel in certain order, had left for Caxamalca where he had heard Atabalipa Inga was. The emissaries caught up with him and gave him the message and the governor (anxious to liberate [Guàscar] and restore his kingdom to him) continued on his way, and Atabalipa was waiting for him with everything in order, which is when the Bishop says that don Francisco Pizarro captured him and killed him and massacred many people, continuing such great cruelties that the friar Marcos de Niza attests to, having been present and a witness to everything.[39] And it could be that this friar Marcos was party to the capturing of the aforementioned Atabalipa and the killing of so many people, because a friar was seen on this occasion with don Francisco Pizarro, named Friar Vicente de Valverde, of the order of Santo Domingo, [who] approached Atabalipa and put a missal in his hands, telling him that it was the holy gospel of God and that he came to preach it to him and to all the land. And he took the book and turned it over in his hands and looked at it, and threw it to the ground like a barbarian; and the good friar, lacking prudence, began to call the Christians to arms, making great exclamations about what he saw. And with this the Spaniards were angered and reached for their arms, and the Indians did the same; with zeal for the service of God, this cleric became involved in this quarrel, being the beginning of it and all the rest.[40] The priests in the countryside and in wars see danger strike and the damage received on both sides, but not the cause and the reason, for the commanders, charged with the remedy and health of their army, only seek advice from those in their war council and skilled in arms, and many times they make a resolution only because it is advisable, and I cannot be persuaded that there has ever been a commander in all the Western Indies who has caused harm, in simple as well as in severe punishments, which the Bishop calls cruelties, who has not been given reason to by the Indians, at times anticipating them and beating them to their evil intentions either in their execution or after

39. The Franciscan Marcos de Niza was not in fact "present and a witness" to these events. He arrived later as a chaplain in the service of Pedro de Alvarado. Vargas Machuca is responding to Niza as cited by Las Casas in the *Brevísima relación*.

40. From all surviving accounts, Vargas Machuca is correct in describing the Dominican Vicente de Valverde's role in inciting the capture of Atawallpa and ensuing massacre. Valverde was the only priest present.

it has happened. As don Luis de Narváez writes in *True Swordplay: The Grandeur of the Sword* (folios 85–86),[41] the swordsman must consider three attacks to understand the foundation of arms: the first, an anticipated [attack]; the second, a simultaneous [attack]; and the third, a counter [attack]; for if he lacks this understanding, his skill will not be complete and he will endanger [himself] in the battle against his opponent. One should take this same advice in war and conquest, and they should be undertaken in the same manner, for if one should acquire and recognize the intention of the enemy, he should attack beforehand; and if he does not have this [knowledge], [he should attack] at the same time or after the first attack; more skill is attributed to the anticipated attack, having recognized the intention [of the adversary]; then the simultaneous [attack] and lastly, the counter attack, due to the danger it poses.[42] These three points apply to the general in war and not to the friars, and these [principles] have been executed in the conquests of the Indies; and primarily the third, the counter attack, has been used and many of our Spaniards have been lost, for when they go to punish, they have received harm; and one might consider the number of Spaniards who have died in diverse parts of the Indies at the hands of the Indians, trusting the false peace that they always offer. And in order to not tire ourselves, note the occasions that the Araucanians in the provinces of Chile have broken [the peace], as we will address in the following chapter.

Once [the events] in Caxamalca were finished, where the conquests of the kingdoms of Peru were begun and the cruelties commenced, as the Bishop says, they continued to conquer the plains and the mountain ranges of Peru, until arriving at the populated city of Cuzco; and returning to the coast of Lima, they peacefully founded the City of the Kings [Lima], which is the seat of the kingdom and provinces of Peru, and all the other plains and mountain ranges with no wars. And if there were any, they were but few and of little consideration, and all the land became quiet and safe, with no reason for punishment or labors for the Indians, until the conspiracies and uprisings began among the Spaniards, as they say, that without them, the Indians would have had no work nor would the Spaniards have given it to them, as they are a people of such kind inclinations that if

41. This classic fencing treatise, *Verdadera destreza: Grandezas de la espada,* was published in Madrid around 1600.

42. Vargas Machuca's swordsmanship metaphors clearly get away from him here.

the truth be known, after the Tascaltecs of New Spain, they are the best in the Indies, and one may give them the title of generous, faithful, thankful, and they love the Spaniards and have been maintained, and they are loved more than others (except those we have mentioned). Reason has this [sort of] strength, as Cicero says (*De Oficiis*, book 1, part xvi); it is the bond for all of human friendship, for there is no other manner in which we differ from brutes, and as far as I know, there is no one so bad that he has nothing to praise. They recognize the benefits gained from the Spaniards and enjoy more freedom than they had with their own lords, who deprived them of what they hunted in order to eat, and from wearing fine blankets, as only the nobles and the privileged could dress as they liked, hunt, and eat freely all they wanted, and these were few, and the rest required particular license; and unheard-of cruelties were found among these heretics,[43] because there was an Inca who, in order to clear the land of useless people, gathered all the lame, one-armed, blind, and old people from his realm and put them into great straw huts and set them on fire. There are some opinions that this happened but once, and others, many times, and though they were pagans, it is great cruelty nevertheless. And so it is true that [the people] have escaped from tyrannies such as those mentioned and others even greater, and because of these [tyrannies] the Incas were lords.[44] And now, they have found the monarchs of Spain to have great clemency and justice, and their ministers and Spaniards much love and kind reciprocity, such as they have had toward them from the first day; the Spanish-speaking natives [*gente ladina*][45] lack no understanding, and there are some who are subtle and quite ingenious; however, we refer to those who cannot speak Spanish well [*bozales*] as barbarians.[46] This is why when a Spaniard wishes to mock someone, he says, "So-and-so is an Indian." One of the Incas in the Kingdom of Peru, a lord over part of

43. Or "among them" (*en ellos; CDI*, 273).

44. It is unclear what source Vargas Machuca is drawing from here, although the sharp turn toward emphasizing Inca tyranny was made by royal cosmographer Pedro Sarmiento de Gamboa, whose 1572 *History of the Incas* was commissioned in Cuzco by Viceroy Francisco de Toledo.

45. Or "dignified people" (*gente digna; CDI*, 273).

46. The term *bozal*, meaning muzzle, was the converse of *gente ladina*, or intelligent and civilized Spanish speakers. According to the 1726 edition of the *Diccionario de la lengua española*, it meant "rustic" and was also a racial epithet for black slaves, especially those who had recently arrived (666).

it, knew this expression quite well, for having received a letter from the viceroy and governor at that time, he called upon a Spaniard to read it to him. When the Spaniard told him he did not know how to read, he responded, "You are as much an Indian as I." If I had to pass judgment, I would switch the nationalities by calling the Indian a Spaniard and the Spaniard an Indian, which he did so keenly.[47] And though I may stray a bit from the purpose, in order to see the inventiveness that some of the lords and caciques have, I will tell what happened to one cacique.

A *mestizo*, son of a Spaniard and an Indian and a people respected by the Spaniards, was passing through his town. An Indian from that town, to whom the *mestizo* owed a hundred pesos, went to the cacique because he could not collect [the debt]. He related his circumstances and asked him to order the [*mestizo*] to pay. The cacique sent a constable to call upon him at the *tanbo* or inn where he was lodged, and when he saw that the cacique was calling upon him and ordering him to appear, he laughed heartily, as any *mestizo* or Spaniard would do, it being an extraordinary thing to convince them [to appear] before Indian justice. And laughing,[48] he responded with harsh words, saying, like a violent brute, that if the cacique wanted anything of him, he should come to the inn himself. Upon receiving the answer, the cacique sent one of the jailers with more than fifty Indians to him, and though he resisted, he was brought in with his hands tied, and they accused him in the presence [of the cacique], where he pompously confessed to the debt. They put him in the stocks and condemned him to pay half his debt before he would be freed, for his being part Indian; and for his other [i.e., Spanish] half, they sent him to the closest Spanish chief magistrate so that justice would be served in the case because of his being part Spaniard. This sentence pronounced, the *mestizo* sent a dispatch to the Royal Audiencia complaining about the cacique; once the case was heard by the judges and well understood, they confirmed the sentence, which was greatly celebrated because the cacique had demonstrated such great subtlety in the case. And if truth be told, some of the Spanish-speaking Indians who have spent time around our Spaniards, both humble

47. It is uncanny how opposite Vargas Machuca's conclusions are to those of his contemporary, Guaman Poma de Ayala, one of the same Peruvians he might classify as "subtle and of great ingeniousness."

48. Or "chastising him" (*riñéndole; CDI*, 274).

and noble, acquire understanding. And returning to my intention, I say that once the Caxamalca [affair] was finished, Atabalipa Inga was sentenced to die because of his denunciation by Filipillo, an Indian [interpreter], and it was proven that he had negotiated and gathered people to kill Spaniards, as well as ordered the death of his brother Guascar Inga, having him killed on the road while bringing him captive to Caxamalca, as we have said, whose death was executed by the captains who were transporting him and fearing that he would reach Caxamalca alive. The governor don Francisco Pizarro knew all the details of his tyranny, from which no advantage nor benefit could result, and with these two deaths Peru was quieted and calmed, which facilitated the conquests. And so, the governor Francisco Pizarro began to dispatch his captains along the two roads in the south, along the plains and the mountain ranges, settling Cuzco and, on the plain, the City of the Kings, also called Lima, and successively many other cities that I do not address [here] as it is unnecessary. At this time he dispatched Captain Benalcázar to the conquest of Quito, which is to the north of Caxamalca, as referred to earlier; this province falls on the same main mountain range of Peru, one degree south of the equinoctial line, a healthy land, abundant and with many natives. When he arrived, he came upon an Indian captain named Ruminagui [Rumiñavi, literally, "Stone-face"], who had taken power as he had heard of the death of Atabalipa Inga, his lord; he rebelled and tyrannized the land and formed his army to defend and oppose the entrance Benalcázar was making. From the first day, Ruminagui had received news that he was coming for him. The two armies gathered and both captains, using all their cunning and stratagems, met many times in different places with great loss of life, more on the part of the Indian than on ours, and Captain Benalcázar always gained ground, and went on to become governor and *adelantado*. He won the land all the way to the principal city of Quito, and there, according to the account by Agustín de Zárate, Benalcázar was told of how Ruminagui, before the city was taken, had gathered together all the women, in great number, and told them, "Now you will all delight, for the Christians are coming, in whom you may take pleasure." And the women laughed, thinking that he said this to be witty, and this laugh was costly, as he ordered them all beheaded, and after this he fled, first setting one of his houses on fire that was full of rich clothing from the time of Guanicapa [Huayna Capac, also spelled Wayna

Kapak], father of Atabalipa Inga who died in Caxamalca, as we
addressed before. [Once he had] entered the city of Quito, he [Benal-
cázar] traveled the land from province to province; some were pacified and subjected on sight, offering no resistance, and others resisted
with great force of arms and fortresses and stockades. Don Diego de
Almagro came from Cuzco to assist, though some chroniclers say
that he went to Túmbes to defend against the entrance of don Pedro
de Alvarado, governor of Guatemala, who he had heard was coming
in discovery of Peru with a great fleet. Once he arrived at Túmbes,
there was no news, and knowing that Captain Benalcázar needed
him in the conquest of Quito, he went to his aid, and once they were
gathered, they subdued the land in a short time; and giving him
the title of governor, he returned to the city of Cuzco, from which
he went on to conquer the Kingdom of Chile, with don Francisco
Pizarro, his companion, governing Peru.

With all of this, I refer to the histories that speak of it, as [their
retelling] is not my intention; I only mention them in order to
demonstrate the ease with which this kingdom was conquered,
from which one may gather that there were no such cruelties as the
Bishop of Chiapa claims, nor a need for severe punishments, and if
there were any, it was due to the urgency given by the natives, as we
mentioned earlier and will address later at length. And it is a solid
truth that the governor Benalcázar peacefully took possession of this
province of Quito and subdued it after the first encounters, and from
that time they have always guarded faith, friendship, and obedience
to His Majesty here, conserving his peace now and for a long time to
come, according to what we may judge of the natives and inhabitants,
by way of divine favor. And the same may be said for the governing
of Popayán, farther to the north, conquered by this same Governor
Benalcázar, or the majority of it, where he earned the title of *adelantado*. Here, though there was native resistance with some skirmishes
and deaths resulting from their defense, there were no punishments
or need for cruelties, and if there were any, they were not of sufficient consideration to [merit] addressing. I confess that from one
end to the other of this province [Popayán], there are very bellicose
Indians everywhere the Spaniards have put their hands, the causes
of which we will address later, in order to first address the famous
Araucanians in the Kingdom of Chile.

*If one were to tell all the particular cruelties and slaughters that the
Christians in those kingdoms of Peru have committed and every day go on
committing, without any doubt they would inspire horror and reprehension,
and so many would there be, that all we have said in other places would be
overpassed and seem small, so many and so grave are they.*
—*Fray Bartolomé de las Casas*

The Fourth Discourse and Defense
Rebuttal and justification of the conquests and pacifications
of the Kingdom of Chile.

Comparatively and *par excellence*, we may call the Indians of the
Kingdom of Chile, in whom neither a faithful spirit nor a trace of
clemency has ever been found, more cruel than the tigers of Hyrca-
nia and the lions of Getulia and the bears of Libya; the reasoning of
Seneca (*De clementia*) applies well: "Cruelty is not typical of men,
but rather of violent brutes, taking pleasure in blood and torments,
leaving human nature behind and turning into wild animals." I have
said much regarding all the Indians referred to, and there is more
to say when we address the New Kingdom of Granada in the next
discourse; and all of this would be unnecessary by simply addressing these Araucanian Indians, for they sufficiently demonstrate our
purpose against the name that the Bishop of Chiapa gives to the
Spaniard, calling him a tyrant and cruel, while calling the Indian
pious and merciful, without many other attributes that he applies
to them and affirms as being true in his treatise. And as omnipotent
God is my witness, I would rather take up the lance against them
than the pen and would therefore better do my duty as a conquering
soldier.[49] I believe that the indubitable reason of any who should read
this discourse would incite him to ire and vengeance; furthermore,
as I have promised full justification and evidence of my intention, I
beg the discreet reader to read with care and consideration, as I am
sure he will find, on the part of the Spaniard, a true defense, zeal-
ously serving God and king, by whose design various strategies and
ruses that the governors who have ruled this kingdom have made use
of are found, not only to end the war without blood but to conserve

49. In 1599, the year he published *The Indian Militia,* Vargas Machuca penned a
plan to conquer the Araucanians, or Mapuche.

the peace as well. By executing [these strategies], they, as well as
their soldiers, have suffered great losses of blood, expecting danger
at every turn until they lose their lives, and cities and estates suffer
great devastation by these deaths; and in these battles, the Indian
pursues victory with a diabolic furor, giving no quarter and with
unheard-of cruelties that they are not moved to cease by religion, nor
decrepit old age, nor youthful ignorance,[50] nor feminine beauty, nor
servile diligence, nor interest in a promised reward, nor the prize of
Heaven, nor the fear of Hell, nor good works, nor braveness of spirit,
nor the desire for nobility and renown. I can only say that they are
driven by a chaotic appetite that at times leads them to do things
that appear to be good; for since God came to the world, no other
nation but this one has been seen that does not find virtue by one
of the known paths, for this [Araucanian nation] has known neither
thankfulness, nor love nor fear, piety nor temperance, shame nor
good will, reason nor request, patience nor pardon, faith nor hope,
pain nor humility, chastity nor desire, compassion nor obedience, and,
above all, no kind of honor nor virtuous act, nor anything of the sort,
except when they move with an unbridled appetite, as we have said.
These Chileans had an overabundance of insolence and cruelty, as
will be seen, of deception, desperation, ire, ingratitude, incredulous-
ness, flattery, lies and maliciousness, idleness and treachery, pride,
suspicion and vengeance, and finally, every sort of vice.

In order to subject this untamable nation, wounded by the influence of an unknown star, it was attacked many times by its own
Incan kings, so famous in the kingdoms of Peru and to whom all
the nations in those lands surrendered and became vassals. The
Araucanians repelled and beat them as many times as they were
attacked, remaining free to rule despotically, without a lord, over
all who would obey them; their government is but leaderless chaos,
divided in many factions and clans, being ruled by the most furious
and determined, and they demonstrate this even today. With the
arrival of the Spaniard, they were to be reduced to servitude, and the
person who placed the yoke of obedience upon them was don Pedro
de Valdivia, beginning this pacification and conquest. They regarded
him more than a human, and thought him and his people to be
immortal, demonstrating their wonder and fright at the horses and

50. Or "youthful innocence" (*inocencia infantil;* CDI, 278).

harquebuses, with which they were restrained for a time until they were no longer deceived by the immortality they attributed to our people. And this friendship would have been more certain and stable if they had not been misled by such thoughts and had been subdued only by the force of arms; for as Cicero says [in *Celium*],[51] deception greatly strains a friendship, for it erases the truth, without which it is false. And these people have shown this well, for they were so taken by this deception that, like so many furious and runaway horses, they took the bit in their teeth and fled to the hills and mountains, gathering together, whereupon they had their councils, made their conspiracies and drunken revelries, preparing their arms and other tools for war, leaving some dead and wounded in order to cement their uprising and rebellion; and so began the war, for insignificant causes, as will be said later. And this war has been so persistent and bloody, such as has never been seen before, sustaining itself unto the present day, and I believe, by what has been seen, that they will sustain it for a long time, that though it is true that some of the governors who have governed that land have been great, famous, and valorous captains, and that with their valor, ruses, and strategies they have resisted and reduced the majority of them to peace, the Indian has always kept his crossbow armed for new rebellions, deaths, and destruction, as will be seen briefly, all because of their evil inclination and unruly appetite, as we have said.

And returning to our purpose, I say, that after don Pedro de Valdivia arrived, he conquered and pacified part of that kingdom, settling the cities of Santiago, seat of that government, La Serena, La Concepción, Imperial, Valdivia, Villa Rica, Angol, Tucapel, and likewise a fort in the Arauca valley and another in Purén, each of these cities being served by the Indians within their boundaries. Fifty-four years ago, more or less, the Indians of Tucapel began to rebel and rise up; the cause of their uprising was [the following]: The aforementioned don Pedro de Valdivia left three *yanaconas* in his service, two blacks, one *mestizo*, and one Spaniard, along with a large number of natives, both male and female, as that is the custom of the land since the females work as much or more than the males, constructing a fort in Tucapel, while he had retired to the city of Concepción. It so happened that while the female Indians were stomping mud, their

51. Possibly *Divinatio in Q. Caecilium.*

clothes tucked out of the way as they usually do (we could say that at that time they go naked, for they only cover their dishonest parts with what they call *panpanillas* [i.e., loincloths], made of cotton and covering them from the waist down about a palm and a half). And at this worksite, on a whim, either the *mestizo* or one of the blacks or *yanaconas* (who it was cannot be verified, not even the Spaniard can be presumed [innocent] as it was such a dishonest and depraved act), ordered them to remove their *panpanillas* so they could carry out this labor and step more freely; clearly this was more out of pleasure and depravity of the person who ordered it than any other thing; and obeying the order, either because they did not know what they were doing or perhaps because they took pleasure in such dishonesty, the Indian females removed them. Soon after, some of their Indian relatives came to the worksite and were insulted to see this, and one lost his composure [and had] words against the *mestizo* who was present, such that the *mestizo* beat him, and the next night the Indians gathered in their council, and before daybreak, they set fire to the fort and all the surrounding structures, killing the Spaniard, the *mestizo,* the blacks, and the *yanaconas.* News of this reached the governor, who, as we said, had retired to Concepción, and he set out to punish [the deed] with fifty-three soldiers and three thousand Indian allies. Marching along the road, he sent six scouts ahead whom the Indians killed in an ambush, leaving their beheaded bodies on the road and retreating to gather strength and more people and to wait for the governor and his soldiers, whom they heard approaching. He arrived to where the bodies were laid out and recognized his losses; but as a valorous captain and brave gentleman, he resolved to advance and give battle to the enemy; and attacking them on an open battlefield, he retreated [only after] having fought a great while, such that the horses were clearly showing their weariness. At that time, a *yanacona* lance squire of don Pedro de Valdivia, called Lautaro, was bringing him a fresh horse and, before being asked to change [horses], saw his people in quick retreat. He spurred the horse and cried out, "Come back! Come back! The victory is yours if you know how to take it! The Spaniards' horses are so tired and wounded they can hardly be turned; and with a little effort you can finish them all off!" The Indians recognized him and, trusting his advice, returned and rejoined the fight. They took the victory promised by Lautaro. In this encounter, the fifty-three Spanish soldiers and the

three thousand Indians died, except for three who escaped and took
the news to Concepción; don Pedro de Valdivia and his confessor, an
ordinary chaplain who was captured along with him, lived for two
days as captives, trying to secure their rescue until an Indian, moved
by his own whim, killed them with a war club against the wishes
of Lautaro, who had just been given the title of field marshal. This
account is quite true, and certain histories that say they were killed
by pouring melted gold into their mouths and making them drink are
only tall tales [like those] of *Amadis* [*of Gaul*].[52] Once this death had
occurred, Lautaro resolved to advance to the city of Concepción, as
he so did, completely destroying it with a million cruelties and havoc,
giving no quarter; and with everything burned and reduced to ashes
he retreated with his army to a place called Mataquito. At that time,
Francisco Villagra, governing the city of Imperial, had received news
of this, and set out for [this place] as captain; and with some soldiers who came from the city of Santiago, he gathered around three
hundred men, and one night, during the morning watch, he attacked
the enemy camp and routed them with many lives lost on both sides.
In this encounter and assault, the famous Lautaro died, of such great
renown in [Alonso de Ercilla's epic poem] *La Araucana*. With this
victory, Francisco de Villagra returned to the city of Imperial from
whence he came. The Indians could easily have avoided this uprising
and rebellion, so much havoc, cruelties, and deaths, for the cause of
it was so minor that, upon receiving news of it, the governor, whose
valor and Christianity were beyond doubt, would have punished [this
crime] with great rigor and justice. Being so cruel, they do not know
what [justice] is, and therefore do not make use of it; and cruelty,
as Pero Mejía says, is the enemy of justice and of all reason and a
sin worse than pride. But, as their nature is so evil and so impious,
without any cause, nothing else could have been expected, and as an
example, the entrance made into the valley of Copiapó at the start of
these conquests should be sufficient [to show] not to trust them at all.

   We know it is true that, after entering his lands, the lord and
cacique named Copiapó offered peace. This valley is named after him,
to whom the unfortunate Valdivia gave so many valuable gifts. And

52.   The reference to the enormously popular chivalric romance *Amadis de Gaula*
is omitted in *CDI* (281). An in-depth study of the influence of Old World fictional texts
on colonial Latin American literature is found in Irving A. Leonard's *Books of the Brave*,
2nd ed. (Berkeley: University of California Press, 1992).

[Copiapó], seeing himself so obliged, and having promised him fitting recompense (though it was later discovered to be a ruse), decided to allow Captain Juan Bohón to remain in that valley along with sixty soldiers. And taking leave of his cacique and friend, strengthening the bonds of friendship with valuable gifts, they had hardly turned their backs when one night all were beheaded and not one escaped, having not any cause in the world with which to conceal or disguise their treason. And this case should be an example of their false friendship, so as to never trust any Indian of the Indies, and particularly in this kingdom, for they surpass all the others in betrayals, cruelties, and vices, as we have explained at length, and as Plato says, perverse is the man who accepts favors but never returns them.

With the unfortunate death of don Pedro de Valdivia leaving that kingdom so troubled by wars (by no fault of his, as he was highly respected while conquering as well as while governing; and as a great gentleman and Christian, he was loved and greatly appreciated by his people, and the Indians [would have felt] the same sense of obligation if their evil nature had not erased it, as will be seen at the end of this discourse), Francisco de Villagra, his appointee, governed in the interim before another was provided. There were several changes that do not serve our purpose, as well as developments in war, but the Marquis of Cañete arrived at the City of the Kings, or Lima, seat of the Kingdom of Peru, to serve as viceroy in those parts. He dispatched don García Mendoza, his son, who later served as viceroy for some years with pomp and powers of governor of this Kingdom of Chile. He arrived there with six hundred Spaniards, among them much nobility from Peru and gentlemen prosperous in estate and valor, and finding the better part of the land in rebellion, began by calling the rebels and insurgents to peace, [to which] they responded with one and many battles. It was the will of God to fill him with his ancient valor, and with a lucky star he fought them with such celebrated victories that he was never said to have had bad luck or misfortune. The Indians recognized this star and valor in this great gentleman, making peace with him out of fear. This generally happened in the entire kingdom, though, as has been said, their crossbows were armed and ready to fire at the first chance, as they so did, and as we will later address. This great gentleman rebuilt all the cities and forts that had been razed and dismantled, and even resettled others. He rebuilt the cities of Concepción, Angol, and Tucapel, as well as the forts in Arauco and Purén, destroyed with the death of Valdivia. He resettled the city of Osorno and, on the other side of the snowy mountains, the cities of Mendoza and San Juan de la Frontera, which stand to this day.

This kingdom enjoyed peace and tranquility while he served, until the time that news arrived that His Majesty Carlos V, of glorious memory, had sent Francisco de Villagra as governor, mentioned earlier. At this time he decided to leave the government [post] and travel to Peru, leaving Rodrigo de Quiroga in his place as governor. He left this kingdom at a good time, no misfortune ever having befallen him, and prudently he did not wish to wait, for as Titus Livy says, nothing should be trusted less than prosperous success, and for success to last, it must be carefully measured, as did don García de Mendoza with his successes, for he had hardly turned his back on the kingdom when the Indians began to rebel, killing their encomenderos for no reason whatsoever, nor [giving] any indication as to why they were moved to such a betrayal, other than simply lacking the strength of the star that followed don García de Mendoza; and they began to cause these deaths with the many reprisals and cruelties they carried in their spirits.

Francisco de Villagra arrived in this kingdom, where he took possession of the government; he found the war had begun and was heated and bloody, so much so that to this day, it [has] always been sought by the Indian, with such great valor and strength, the only two qualities that heaven has given them; and this cannot be denied, for this has been seen by experience, so long has the war here lasted, with great loss and damage to our own, having no relief, for harm always reaches the majority. And though it has happened in this way, they have resisted with valor, and I believe they would do it for a long time, according to the means that our side has used so moderately. This sore is cancerous and needs strong and severe caustics, for we know that gentleness means nothing to these people. This governor conducted the war during his government with great valor and bravery, and though he was a great captain with much experience, he had many losses and several victories in that war, until Concepción, Tucapel, Arauco, and Purén were abandoned for the second time.[53]

---

53. The Royal Palace transcription mentions Francisco de Villagra's death at this point (*CDI*, 284).

His successor was Pedro de Villagra, also a great and experienced soldier, and after him, Rodrigo de Quiroga, who accomplished several things, rebuilding Concepción and Tucapel in a few places. The Royal Audiencia succeeded him, presided over and governed by the licentiate Bravo de Saravía, who personally took part in the war for a long time, as well as his field marshal and captains. During this time, they experienced several losses, the Indians burning Tucapel and the forts at Arauco and Purén for the third time, leaving everything desolate. With these different events, several governors entered and left the kingdom. In the middle of all this, the captain Francis Drake entered the South Sea; with this news and warning, King Philip II, of glorious memory, dispatched don Alonso de Sotomayor, a knight of the Order of Santiago, to defend the kingdom with a force of people and royal powers, because of the great reputation his person possessed. He left Spain as quickly and briefly as possible in the year 1581 in the convoy fleet under Diego Flores de Valdés, with orders to establish settlements [along] the Strait of Magellan. Because of great storms and losses of ships and people, he [Valdés] was unable to sail farther [south] than forty-two degrees, returning to Brazil where don Alonso de Sotomayor wintered. Before these storms, he had taken the fleet and people up the Plate River, quite happy and with good fortune, as he always had. Arriving at Buenos Aires, his people landed and, provided with all necessities, crossed the plains of Paraguay and Tucumán, opening new roads, as the region from the Plate River to the Kingdom of Chile was unknown and impassable; knowledge of that land was confusing, and he and his men suffered many labors, hunger, and danger because of it. For more than seven months he traveled these desolate roads, finally arriving in Chile with 430 soldiers, good people, but without those who died at sea and on the land, overcome by illness. Arriving and finding the war well under way, with many losses on our side, he took possession of the government and continued the war for ten years without ceasing, but with many skirmishes, battles, and assaults, emerging victorious always with good fortune and without any notable defeats, for other than the soldiers who died in that war with their weapons in their hands, few, if any, were captured or killed; no town was ravaged or burned, but rather a great number of natives were brought to peace, such as in the boundaries of Villa Rica, Valdivia, Osorno, Castro, and those of Imperial, Angol, and Chillán, in the snowy mountains, with many deaths and [much] weakening of the enemy. This star so fair would follow him to the end of his governance, leaving no opportunity for the Indians to employ their ancient custom of greedily bathing their hands in our blood with cruelties, past and yet to come.

As proof of the great virtue and valor and knowledge of war in those parts, from the first day, [Sotomayor] was thought of as having the experience of his whole life in that kingdom, for Plutarch writes that the art of war is shown by the one who uses it most, and Titus Livy says that the judge of war is its outcome, and so, according to this, each is judged by the outcome he had; and neither in the middle nor at the outset did he fail, but rather had many good, prosperous, and admirable triumphs; nor was he ever judged by what his many soldiers said; we may say that his star was recognized because of the effects, after divine favor. I will tell what a soldier of his related to me to prove this: that having pacified the territories belonging to the cities of Valdivia, Osorno, and Villa Rica, and a large portion of Imperial, as well as Angol and Chillán, as mentioned, he made the majority of the Indians, by rigor of war, to come down from the mountains and settle on the plains where instructed. Once their houses and planting fields were established, and with no obligation of servitude whatsoever, they asked him to build a fort in the Purén Valley to better keep the peace and make the rest come, and so that the enemy would not go there, nor to the swamps nearby, and make war upon them and displace them. And because of this request, he vowed to assist them and began [construction]. And seeing that he was committed and the work had begun, with a diabolic spirit (having prepared arms and other war supplies in the interim), [the Indians] rebelled. So as to not lose any opportunity, they had first made an agreement with the peaceful Indians serving the city of Angol to advise them when the city lacked enough people for its defense, and with the majority of the inhabitants and their governor in the fort, they advanced, and three thousand Indians immediately gathered and, with other confederates, marched upon the city of Angol, attacking it in a surprise assault and setting it afire in four places. And God had prepared assistance, as it so happened that that night, during the first watch, the governor arrived [at the city] from the aforementioned fort being built in the Purén Valley, with sixty soldiers in his company he had taken with him by chance. He was heard to have said, as he went to bed, "God be blessed, tonight I will sleep safe and sound," and he fell asleep with this pleasant thought. And at the first sign of sleep the enemy was entering the city, as we mentioned, setting all four corners on fire, and the largest group of people happened to reach the house of the valiant Cañuman, of such fame in *La Araucana*, who arose and, taking up his lance, began to cry out, saying, "Ah! Traitors! Here I am, the *apo* [lord] who will take his revenge of you!" And though he was old, he demonstrated his venerable bravery well with his lance, and held them off for a long while, and they were taken aback upon recognizing him. And news had reached the governor and every sector was called to arms, and he and his people fought their way to where the valiant old man resisted and where the enemy was the strongest; and having sent his people to defend the other places where necessary, he joined the fray with great strength and on all sides, protected by his enduring valor and the strength of valiant soldiers such as those who followed him that day; and they repelled the enemy in a short time, causing them to flee and chasing after them for six leagues, but as the night was so dark they were unable to find the main group as they had scattered. Later, however, by day, they came upon a group of two hundred Indians and killed or captured the majority of them in the encounter. Those who remained in the city had much to do to extinguish the fire, which had furiously spread to all parts.

The Bishop of Chiapa would easily see here the scant faith of these native Indians, for they had asked that the aforementioned fort be built, with all enthusiasm and happiness, to be protected against the Indians in war, and they themselves were among those who lit the fires, coming to their aid and believing that by destroying this city the fort would also easily fall. I am certain that this lack of trust is easily recognized, and whoever should not see it, I beg him to read ahead in this discourse, where he will find certain disillusion when we address Martín García de Loyola, knight of the Order of Calatrava, with whom we will demonstrate and bring to a close all that we have said of these Indians, that they possess no qualities other than bravery and strength, as we have said. This strength is so great that to demonstrate it I will but tell of the Purén Valley, in a skirmish that the governor and his soldiers joined with the enemy, an Indian ran his lance completely through the body of one of his soldiers, Alonso Sánchez, who was armed with two coats of mail and a leather buff-coat, which is equal to six doublets; and they saw the better part of the lance pass through his body; and wanting to satisfy their curiosity regarding the fabrication of the metal lance head, they found that it was a sharpened dagger that had been taken by killing a Spaniard in a previous encounter.

After ten years of the government of don Alonso de Sotomayor, as we have said, he traveled to Peru to meet with the viceroy don García de Mendoza in order to put an end to this war. All the Kingdom of Chile expected that he would end the war much faster than any other person at the time, and that the viceroy would provide assistance from Peru with a large number of people, arms, munitions, and other provisions. And assuming he would return supplied with all he desired, his line of thinking was cut short by fortune, for upon his arrival to the City of the Kings [Lima], he received the news of what His Majesty had provided for Martín García de Loyola, because he was no longer governor [of Chile], and because the new [governor, García de Loyola,] immediately left for Chile and took possession of those provinces,[54] where he began to make war with them in a manner quite distinct from that required by the evil character of the Indians. This nobleman was married to a woman, granddaughter of the Incan king and lord of all the kingdoms of Peru, who was called La Coya [Quechua for "Princess" or "Queen"], and in general, the Indians respected her as such, as if we were to call her the Lady of the land. And it seemed to him that this wedding would obligate them to obey him, with no manner of betrayal, as he made known to all the Indians in the various and diverse parliaments he had with them, and the Indians, who were all well informed, told him that he was their true *apo*, and as such, he would see that they would always obey him. With these words and other suspicious acts, veiled in servitude and humility, he was obliged to treat them with the gentlest means possible, occupying the time with the favors he gave them, promising them more liberty than what they presently enjoyed; and as this was so favorable to them, they accepted him, and he saw that in this manner they all would serve, as was soon seen in their work. Believing all of this, the good gentleman valued industry much more than arms, and so began to neglect them, giving license and permitting many valiant soldiers to leave that kingdom, jeopardizing the protection of

54. The Royal Palace transcription relates how Loyola kissed Sotomayor's hands before leaving for Chile (*CDI*, 288).

several experienced captains he had, communicating with the Indians as openly as if there had been fifty years of peace; this could not have been presumed nor expected from them if what Cassian states is true, that true peace is having harmony with good manners and warring against vice;[55] therefore one cannot believe that it was a true peace with these people, as they entirely repudiate this statement; and they should know this [statement] as well, in the words of Sallust, that war is the cause of peace, and it cannot be kept with different inter-pretations and diverse opinions. With this subtle communication, they were making off with many horses and livestock, and when they were well-stocked, they began killing Indian allies and Spanish soldiers. Seeing that no punishment was done and that they lived in complete confidence, that they were trusted and any apology was accepted, the faithful thief being treated with patience, and hiding from them the excesses and deaths they caused, their malice and evil nature were such that, waiting for the right occasion, they killed [Loyola] along with more than fifty of his finest captains and soldiers, drunkenly celebrating with the head of this unfortunate gentleman. With this deed, almost the entire land rose up in rebellion, killing in its wake more than five hundred Spanish soldiers with bitter cruelty; and as if they were victorious, they laid waste to, destroyed, and razed everything they came upon, burning cities, churches, and mon-asteries and killing and making martyrs of priests, forgiving none no matter how young, as long as the fury of their arms lasted. Once that rebellion had ended, they captured several women and took them away, forcing nothing upon them other than their barbarous appetite, that they always obey without faith or reason, as seen by the acts described previously. As St. Bernard says, faith knows no ugliness, it understands what reason cannot, it comprehends the obscure, embraces the immense, understands the future, and encloses within itself all eternity. This virtuous gentleman died, and virtue is such a loyal friend that it accompanies us unto death, and this can be seen here, as in the end the enemy confessed, for once he died, an Indian came from afar, having heard of his death, lamenting and crying out, saying, "What have you done? Are you so drunk that you have killed our father? Now you can expect nothing but labor, affliction, misfortune, and death!" We may say that his was a true prediction,

---

55. Cassian is St. Cassianus, or John Cassian, an early fifth-century monastic writer; the reference is to *The Conferences,* conference 11: "On Perfection."

and, as it is seeming to say at this point, there is no one so evil that he does not have some good, and I confess it is so, nor so good that he does not possess some evil. Virtue is so strong it summons us, even through our enemies, as virtue summoned this good gentleman. I am not sure if the Bishop don Fray Bartolomé would be satisfied by this, because of the deception that so lorded over his thoughts; it is a clear deception to accept man for what he can never be.

And they tortured him [the cacique Bogotá] with the strappado and then
they poured boiling fat upon his belly, shackled him by his feet to irons
atop one stake, with his neck bound to another, and two men tugging at his
hands, and while he was in this position they held fire to his feet; and the
tyrant [Jiménez de Quesada] would enter from time to time and tell him
that he would die in that wise, little by little, by torture, if he did not give up
the gold. And the captain kept his word and killed this lord with tortures.
—Fray Bartolomé de las Casas

The Fifth Discourse and Defense
Rebuttal and justification of the conquests of
the New Kingdom of Granada.

Obeying reason is freedom of the spirit, for [the spirit] chooses that
which seems reasonable; and obeying and defending [reason] is not
freedom of the mind, as this must be subjected to reason in all of its
operations, without exceeding its limitations. For these reasons, I find
myself forced to prove that the deed of the conquests of the Indies
does not deserve to be called tyrannical or cruel, as the Bishop would
have it; and because in this proof we have addressed primarily the
Windward and Leeward isles, the Northern Sea, Tierra Firme and
New Spain, Peru, and Chile, which were the first kingdoms in the
Western Indies the Spaniards discovered and conquered,[56] now, for
dessert, we will address the New Kingdom of Granada to make our
defense, as we find sufficient examples and reasons for that which
we wish to defend. This was the third kingdom discovered and where
the most recent and continuous wars and conquests have taken place;
they have lasted up to the present day and will continue for many
years to come, so it will be necessary for us to lengthen the history
and justification [of the conquests], concluding so as to hear the initial judgment in this world and a second judgment in the next, and to
denounce, first and before all other things, the Bishop and his fitness
to act as judge, and to object to his role of accuser, for the things he
narrates in his treatise differ so greatly from what actually happens now and [happened] in the past, that we are forced to consider
him full of passion and too easily giving credit to so many sinister
deeds that he considered, making them just and true and supporting

56. Or "defended" (*defendieron; CDI,* 291).

them with his authority. And whether they are or not, those who are experienced in that land will see it as easily as I, for his treatise has so many well-known errors that there is no one who would not recognize them and deduce the rest. And if those who do not have this experience wish to consider his accusations and this defense, they will also notice that there is not only one deception but many, for though deception may have a goodly hue, as Aristotle says against Anaxagoras, it is natural that to one deception is attached another and another, so that once the first is revealed, so are the rest.

To the point, then, let us look at who discovered this New Kingdom of Granada, and what wars were fought there and the cruelties he and later conquerors committed, all of which happened beginning in the year 1539 [1537], when it was settled by don Gonzalo Ximenez de Quijada [Jiménez de Quesada]. Having traveled up the great Magdalena River, with great fatigue and labors as it was such a long and tedious journey of more than 200 leagues, through poor lands, ill and quite hot, with great plagues of mosquitoes and little food, all [being] forest and jungles, having no guide whatsoever other than divine providence, coming across so many and great rivers dividing right and left, he always managed to take the right course in order to arrive at the kingdom. And this continuous struggle in route finding continued until they found a sign of healthy land, arriving, by divine favor, at a river they call the Carare, flowing from the provinces of the Muzos. Six or eight days upstream, they went ashore on the left bank (the right choice, for if they had disembarked on the right bank it would have been wrong), so that there was no chance of their getting lost because they were in the provinces of Indians called Muzos, just mentioned, man-eating savages with an herb so plentiful and venomous that, without a doubt, none would escape. Here, it is known that God was the guide, as he was in the conquests of New Spain and Peru, guiding and favoring our side in the first encounters. Going ashore, they found some small paths, which they followed; and though the forests were so great and so dense, in four days they came upon open and level land called savannahs and the road grew wider there; and in another four days they came upon great populations of Indians who had already received news of their coming, and with the admiration of seeing such strange-looking people, the headmen among them gathered together, and unanimously agreed to welcome and receive them, as they so did. This general had left [the coast] with 1,000 soldiers, but he entered this land with 160 soldiers, half of whom were ill, while the rest had died along the road of illness and starvation from such a long journey. Here they recuperated from their labors and calamities, for as Plato says [in *The Republic*, book 2, and *Timaeus*], God is always the source of good and not of evil. And this was clear, as it was His will that these Indians appeared upon their arrival in this land so they could recover, showing themselves to be so humble and of such a fine disposition that they cured them of their ills more than if they had been their own children. At first they brought them eight- and ten-year-old boys to eat, but as they saw that [the Spaniards] did not eat human flesh, they brought them deer; and as they ate this, they continued to bring this along with fruits and tubers from the land, and just as much each day. The general was informed of the existence of as many people, ten, fifteen, and twenty leagues away in that kingdom, and seeing his soldiers recuperated, he settled a city there with the permission and desire of the caciques, calling it Vélez, having previously discovered and settled the city of Santa Fe, in the province of Bogotá, the most famous in all those provinces and [new] kingdom.

Here, in this city of Vélez, there were no [Spanish] cruelties, and the Indians never gave cause for them, nor for punishment, because they sustained and always kept peace and faith. Fewer than two leagues from this city there is a river, and in it there is a rocky outcrop with a smooth, flat face, and carved upon this face there is a cross, and I have seen it. This general wanted to know the secret [of this cross], amazed to have discovered it, and he was told by very old Indians how their fathers and ancestors knew of it, passing it down for more than 1,500 years, according to the number of moons they counted, as if they were months, for they have no other way of [marking time]. [They told] how a man with a long beard passed through that land, and his clothing was the same as theirs, and he looked similar, in his hair, clothing, and shoes (if anyone wore them), to the way the Apostles are depicted, and if there is any difference it is small; and [they told of] how in his hand he carried an insignia similar to that found on the rock, which he himself inscribed with the fingernail of his right hand, and of how he tried to give them a new doctrine, different from the one they had, and because they did not receive it, he left, telling them that there would come a time when they would see all their land possessed by a foreign people who followed the doctrine and religion that he preached to them; and they are certain that this time had come with the arrival of the Christians, and that all should be of one doctrine and law. And though it is true that we have no divine or human scripture that tells us that the Apostles crossed to the Western Indies, one may piously believe that they, or some of their disciples, went to preach the Holy Gospel, and this indication and sign is evident, along with others that have been discovered, though they do not follow this faith.[57] Montezuma and Atabalipa and other ancient lords have said that they were told by their idols that Christians would settle in their lands. And it is not strange that the Devil would foretell this, for as such a great knower of scripture he could have known that it was predicted by the prophet Abdias [Obadiah] in the transmigration of Jerusalem, in the word *bosfor* [Bosphorus]. And defining this place, the Learned Maestro Friar Luis de León says that the word *bosfor* is understood to mean the Strait of Gibraltar, and the same prophet later says that from this strait, or *bosfor,* which mean the same, angels carried the Gospel to the cities of the South, which are our Indies, and that there they would preach to a naked, scorned people with no beards on their faces. And he described the lands and their disposition as one who spoke with the light of the Holy Spirit. One may see this place explained and confirmed in the treatise he wrote about the prophet Abdias.[58] So it appears to be divine will, shown by so many miracles that God has caused in aid to our [people] in their incursions and in their encounters, aided in some places by Our Lady, and in others by the Lord Santiago [St. James], patron of Spain, such as seen in Chile, aided by the Mother of God who prevented that kingdom from being abandoned and all of our [people] from perishing. Considering the conquests of these three kingdoms together, New Spain, Peru, and the New Kingdom of Granada, we will find that entrance into each

57. The Spanish alleged to have heard many versions of this tale in the Americas, and usually claimed that St. Thomas was responsible. For New Granada, see J. Michael Francis, "Language and the 'True Conversion' to the Holy Faith: A Document from the Archivium Romanus Societatis Iesu, Rome, Italy," *The Americas* 62:3 (2006): 445–53.

58. León's treatise is entitled *In Abdiam Prophetam* (published in 1589). The Jesuit José de Acosta, in his ca. 1590 *Natural and Moral History of the Indies,* book 1, chap. 15, says almost the same thing as Vargas Machuca on this point, suggesting he may have picked up these ideas here. See Acosta's *Natural and Moral History of the Indies,* ed. Jane Mangan, trans. Frances López-Morillas (Durham: Duke University Press, 1998), 49.

one was provided to us by the will of God who favored our purpose, guiding and helping us, with weapons in hand against the natives and with sustenance and service. From this we understand that the conquests and conquerors are not a disservice to God, as the Bishop argues with such great passion.

And returning to our purpose, we know that [Jiménez de Quesada] entered the valley of Bogotá, with some of the first Indians who helped and served him, as well as the first important cacique he met, who was Suesca, and pacified his land, followed by the largest of all, which was Bogotá, where the city of Santa Fe, the seat of that kingdom, was founded. And later, successively, Chía, Cajicá, and Ontivon [Fontibón], and the other neighboring towns, which were a great number. And having returned to the first Indians he had met, they settled [in their land], as has been said, in the city of Vélez. These Indians were unfortunate not to have been free like the Indians of Puná in Peru and the Tascaltecs in New Spain, by following them willfully[59] and with reason; as far as I can tell, they were not [free] because there were many caciques and native lords who ruled that land, whereas in Puná there was no more than one, and if there were more in Tascala, they were powerful, and in these Indians of the city of Vélez this did not occur for there was no [single] cacique who took control, and neither did the Spaniards or [some indigenous] governor, as there were so many lords and caciques ruling over so few. In addition, as they were not involved in any wars, they did not seem to be as [warlike] as the others, nor was their labor of any consideration that they would have been obligated to it. He then set out to found the city of Tunja and on the way pacified Guatavita, Choconta, and Turmequé, and the cacique Sodamoso [Sogamoso], of great power and fame; and many cities in this New Kingdom were successively founded, all without any kind of war as it was unnecessary, except for those in the torrid lands, as we will see later.[60] Where there was no war, we may correctly believe that there were no [Spanish] cruelties or punishments, nor any reduction of the Indians, and the distribution and totals we made in New Spain regarding their multiplying

59. Or "in goodness" (*bondad;* CDI, 295).

60. For a clearer version of these events, plus testimony from the conquerors, see J. Michael Francis, ed., *Invading Colombia: Spanish Accounts of the Gonzalo Jiménez de Quesada Expedition of Conquest* (University Park: Pennsylvania State University Press, 2007).

[i.e., in population] should be noted, as it may be shown that there was no diminishing, nor was the land depopulated by wars and cruelties as the Bishop claims. For it is well known, and generally certain, that in this land I have referred to there was no war whatsoever, and it is as populated today as it was when the Spaniards entered, and even more so with the aforementioned multiplying, as it seems in the town of Bosa and many others, in which a greater abundance of vassals is now found than when our [people] entered these provinces.[61] [The Bishop] claims that cruelties were committed because the Indians did not give up the gold and emeralds and other precious stones they had, and for these reasons, this general committed [cruelties] on many different occasions. What I can say of this general, who was, as has been said, don Gonzalo Jiménez de Quesada (made *adelantado* in that kingdom by the King for his services), [is that he] found himself with his army in the towns of [cacique] Suesca because a soldier took a blanket from an Indian and demanded gold; [despite] having so few Spaniards with him, he had [the soldier] hanged. This was not the spirit of a cruel man, for if it were, he would have given many things to keep from losing a soldier, since there was no assistance to make up for the lack of soldiers.

[The Bishop] says there were precious stones and emeralds, and that for this reason the Indians were pressured. At that time, there were none in that or any other kingdom, except in the provinces of the Muzos, at a mountain called Itoco, and they were not discovered for more than thirty years after that kingdom was conquered, nor were there any other precious stones. And if there are any now in other places in that kingdom, in Somondoco or in Peru, in Puerto Viejo [Ecuador], they are not worked nor will they ever be, such that cruelties cannot have been committed for emeralds and precious stones at the time the Bishop claims.[62]

Afterwards, they settled Tocaima and Vague [Ibagué], Mariquita, Muzo and La Palma, Pamplona and Mérida, Neiva and the town of

61. Vargas Machuca's claim of population growth under Spanish rule is absurd. See J. Michael Francis, "Población, enfermedad y cambio demográfico, 1537–1636: Demografía histórica de Tunja, una mirada crítica," *Fronteras de la Historia* 7 (2002): 15–95.

62. This is another absurd claim, as the discovery of emeralds at Somondoco was described by Jiménez de Quesada and many others. See Francis, *Invading Colombia*, 62, 71, 98. For the Muzo conquests and discoveries, see Kris Lane, *Colour of Paradise: The Emerald in the Age of Gunpowder Empires* (New Haven: Yale University Press, 2010), chap. 2.

La Plata and that of Los Angeles, Timaná and other towns; the Muzos and [the native peoples of] La Palma, Mariquita, and all the towns of the Neiva Valley, which are all in torrid lands, broke the peace, and the war began with such great severity that it cost many lives on both sides, as they were such a bellicose people. In some places it ended quickly, but in others it lasted for a time, and in others still, it has lasted to this day and will continue. In these hot lands, the [numbers of] Indians have been diminished for the reasons mentioned; on the isle of Santo Domingo, in wars and when they retreat into the forests, they are afflicted by hunger and sickness, and after they are reduced to peace, some go to serve in the cities in temperate lands (that we call cold). This is, in part, one of the reasons that in some provinces where there once were four [Indians], only two or fewer remain, and this count and number [i.e., rate of decline] has occurred in all the torrid lands, whereas in the cold lands, the population growth is comparable to that referred to in New Spain.

A captain named Pedro de Ursúa entered to conquer the land of the Muzos, and it was he who was killed by the tyrant Lope de Aguirre on the Marañón [River].[63] This commander, finding himself in this province and having made peace with the caciques and native lords there, settled the city of Tudela; and as the entire land had rebelled against him and several of his soldiers were killed, he wished to punish the land; and [the Muzos] so harassed him with their arms that he was forced to abandon and leave it with more than half of his people wounded or dead, for the land was quite rugged and the natives were warlike and great warriors and made use of twenty-four-hour herb venom. After some time, the captain Luis Lanchero, principal nobleman of that kingdom, finding himself somewhat more comfortable than the other [captain], went, with authority of the Royal Audiencia, to punish a town of Indians that was close to the Muzos, called Susa, well-provided with people and other supplies necessary to settle the aforementioned ruined city, [Tudela]. And meeting resistance from the natives upon arriving, he did not think it was opportune, and so went some four leagues ahead and, finding advantageous circumstances, settled the city of Trinidad with the renewed consent of the caciques and native lords who had already made peace for the second

63. On Ursúa and the subsequent conquest of Muzo, see Fray Pedro de Aguado, *Recopilación historial*, ed. Juan Friede, 4 vols. (Bogotá: Biblioteca de la Presidencia de Colombia, 1956), 2:205–67 (orig. published ca. 1581).

time. But not forgetting their evil nature and inclination, not many days passed before they rose up, having caused the deaths of some Spaniards outside the city, and naturally retreating to strong positions. Here, the commander and soldiers saw their malicious peace and went out by land to punish them; and in order to do this and capture the caciques and the guilty ones, they found it necessary to wield their arms, as the Indian committed a true act of war, and the [ensuing] dispute, pacification, and punishment was not so inconsequential that it did not last many days and years, and a great many people from both sides died in it; and the natives gathered themselves together in such a manner that in more than twenty-five years the land was not pacified completely, for when one province kept a malicious peace another kept a proper war, so all this time there were always new causes for punishments, for no cacique rebelled without first killing Spaniards, lighting fires, and burning churches, and the last punishment made, of the cacique Guazara, was executed by myself, as I said before. These Indians ate human flesh, which is why they were, and are, so warlike; they are a people who use arrows and a foul, potent herb, more [poisonous] than any other known of anywhere; and these have been the reason such a great number of our Spaniards have died in the pacifications. They use [the poison] on their arrows and the barbs that they place on the paths in order to wound the feet, as well as on spikes in holes hidden under the ground that cave in under those who walk over them, wounding them in their chests; and they also put them among the branches of trees. Here, seeing themselves so wounded by the venom and the Indians so indomitable, and so greatly cunning and treacherous, the Spaniards began to take advantage of dogs, already used in the war of Guali and in other places for the same reasons, and the method of using them was so profitable, as we have already stated, that the fruits were quickly recognized. And it occurred to the Indians, seeing this use of dogs, to destroy all the food from the land and not to plant, sustaining themselves on wild roots and fruit so that the conquerors would be forced to abandon [the land] out of necessity and hunger; and as this experiment lasted for two years or more, they themselves died in great numbers of hunger and illness in the forests; and recognizing their own difficulties, and that the Spaniard had assistance from various sources, they agreed to sow and cultivate the land again so that all could eat and go to war, as they so did; and if they used to sow one *fanega* [approximately 1.5 bushels] they would sow two from now on, one reserved for our soldiers. Since the beginning of time such a thing has never been seen nor heard, that one nation should occupy itself in sowing crops specifically for the enemy, against whom and at all times they fight and make war. The Spaniards were told of this resolution, that they did not wish them to lack any food whatsoever so that they could go to war until either one or the other emerged victorious; and this was their intention in generally conserving their crops. Our [people] accepted the gesture, and so observed it. This demonstrated great courage and strength, such that our side began to doubt the immediate pacification of those provinces; but in the end, as each day brought us new aid and their [side] was weakening, over the course of time they began to be subdued. But during this time, whoever may ponder the church burnings, and the deaths of Spaniards that the Indians sought with such strange cruelties, should not be surprised that our [people] use severe and extraordinary punishments upon a people so evil and bloodthirsty. In this same way, or similarly, most of the pacifications have occurred.

Look, now, at the meekness of the Indians and the cruelty of our [people], as the Bishop says, slandering his nation and generally confessing that there was never any conqueror who was not, or is not, a tyrant and cruel; moreover, as in law, where the complete and utter denial, or dubious confession of anything, is received as a clear indication of any deed, the confession and declaration [the Bishop] made will not cause damage, even though it has been such that there are no foreign nations who do not consider Spaniards the most cruel in the world. Indeed, I have seen in France, in the city of Paris, canvases painted with the cruelties that the Bishop writes of in his book, and not only have I seen the paintings, but [I have seen them] brought forward to show the scandal that this treatise has caused, exaggerating and propagating the deed, and this has come to be multiplied in the pictures and relations written within, in such a manner that as composed as a man could be, I doubt that he would not lose some of his patience; but as patience is a companion to wisdom, as St. Augustine says (*De Sap.* chapter 2), each man will possess it according to his talents.

In these provinces, the Indians are of such a nature that they hang themselves for any trouble they have received, and thus many die in this manner. Here they make great use of venom, and with it they have killed many of our people; it was quite common in wartime to find human flesh, from the soldiers, cooking in pots in their houses, and one hungry soldier managed to eat from one of these pots, only to discover a hand and foot, possibly of his comrade. One should not forget that here in this province and city of the Muzos, called Trinidad, the deception we mentioned occurred, which we will not repeat so as to return to address the New Kingdom, within which the natives possess the worst nature in all the Indies; such that, if they were bellicose, as the Muzos just mentioned, [it would have been] impossible to reduce them to peace, at least a great number of them; but God provided that they should lack such brave spirit; their incli- nation is to be but merchants, and they are so subtle in their dealings, that there are no marked Jews[64] that are more so, which is why they are peaceful and more tame than others in those parts, such as those of Quito and those provinces, for they made almost no war against the Spaniards who settled there and made them subjects, and if they did, it was little or insignificant. Here and there, most of them take part in drunken revelries and they are great herbalists and sorcerers and shamans; they have great sanctuaries under the earth containing a wealth of gold, which some *santeros* [shamans] have been coerced and pressed to reveal; but they are of such condition that they would rather die broken in many pieces before they would do such a thing, for they would rather obey the orders of the Devil rather than look to their own good or that of the Christian, and if they have received any harm from the Spaniards it was for this reason: first, to make sure there are no temples nor adoration of the demon; and second, to make all the treasure the Devil has there, along with so much idola- try, useful to this world; and I believe that the Bishop must not have come across any [such] sanctuary while he walked these lands, for if he had, I am certain that his great Christianity would procure to destroy it and prevent the idolatry and sacrifices that are made there, and he would remove the gold and decorate the temples with it, so that this treasure that had once been dedicated to the worship of the Devil be converted for that of our true God, or he would give it to the poor or donate it to some hospital.

64. *Judíos de señal.* In earlier times, Jews remaining in Spain were permitted to live among Christians if they wore some sign on their clothing that identified them as such (*Diccionario de la lengua española*, 22nd edition). The Royal Palace transcription reads "marked *Indians*" (CDI, 300).

The Spaniards have also caused some harm due to the negligence of several inexperienced judges in those kingdoms, whom we call greenhorns, since they arrive from Spain with no understanding of the natives of those places, and wish to bestow such favor on them, neglecting the Spaniards and believing that in this way they [i.e., the Indians] will be brought to virtue. With these favors, they lose respect for God and the King, rebelling, causing a million deaths and notable effronteries, so that when they realize the damage, these judges are stopped short and the remedy always arrives too late. And putting aside the uprisings and deaths that have occurred so often because of this, I will recount a case that happened among these Indians that serves as an example of [our] purpose, without the other thousand that have occurred throughout the entire Indies.

It concerns a soldier who was in a town called Hontibon [Fontibón], two leagues from the city of Santa Fe [de Bogotá], the seat of that kingdom and location of the Royal Audiencia, and who had a certain difference [of opinion] with an Indian and struck him a few times, and this Indian cried out and the entire town gathered and came to his defense. Seeing himself surrounded by so many, the soldier reached for his sword but, unable to defend himself against such a multitude, he was subdued and, tying his hands and feet and terribly mistreating his person, they decided to put him on a horse and take him to the [audiencia] president. Once before him, [the president] verbally berated him, put him in jail, gave him a fine, and later released him without reprimanding the Indians for their outrage; this is where they begin to lose their respect and their fear, the root of their rebellion, for as Democritus says, daring begins the deed. And the damage done by the soldier could have been avoided had he exercised prudence, for when [the soldier] was freed, insulted by the case, he readied a horse and money and bought a crossbow with fifty bolts; and waiting for the full moon in order to enjoy its advantage, one night, at the first watch, he left the city, passed through this same town of Hontibon two leagues away, and stopped upon a bridge over a river, one league farther on the road to Peru. He tied his horse there and questioned every Indian that passed; as the weather is mild there and night was clear, people[65] constantly passed by on their way to their farms, crops and livestock; and if one arrived

65. The Royal Palace transcription reads "Indios" (*CDI*, 302). The Salamanca manuscript has this crossed out, with "gente" written above (folio 160).

alone, he did not let him [pass], but, with his crossbow loaded, he would demand, "Jaiba," which means "Where are you from?" and if the Indian responded, "From Hontibon," he shot a bolt through him (he always had one ready when [an Indian] arrived), and when he fell, [the soldier] would throw him into the river; and if the Indian named a different place, he would let him pass. He continued in this manner almost the whole night, until he had no more bolts left, and seeing that he still had more time as well as more Indians, he resorted to using his sword until he bloodied it well. And seeing that the day was breaking, he threw the crossbow into the river, mounted his horse, and took the road to Peru. When the punishment was discovered the next day, the president was notified and an investigation was made; [by the time] they realized that it could have been the soldier, he already had a two-day lead, sufficient time for him to have left the kingdom with no chance of catching up to him, especially since he did not sleep day or night. He escaped and the town greatly suffered and the entire kingdom was quite terrified with the case, something that the president could have avoided by punishing the Indians for their outrage and shamelessness, greater in those lands than in Spain [when] laborers mistreat a lord of vassals and of title, and by arresting the Spaniard for several days until his ire passed, as if it were a punishment, but without giving him any other penalty. Seeing the Indians punished in this way, the soldier would have had no evil thoughts, and all the damage that was done would have been stopped short at the beginning. As Livy says (*Lib. 8, dec. 1*), much damage and evil comes from not punishing in a just and timely manner; as it happened in these rebellions, with frivolous punishments at the outset, they soon become greater.

And if the ideas of the Bishop had been followed, there would not have been one Spaniard left alive in all the Indies, both because of his great piety and the evil nature of the Indian, as we can see for example in many provinces that are in rebellion and are more cruel than the first day; and this because of carelessness and lack of timely punishment, as in the province of the Pijaos, where so many Spanish towns have been destroyed and emptied of people because of the harm and cruelty they have done.[66] And if the Bishop were alive, it

66. On the Pijao wars, see Fray Pedro Simón, *Noticias historiales,* and Alvaro Félix Bolaños, *Barbarie y canibalismo en la retórica colonial de los indios Pijaos de Fray Pedro Simón* (Bogotá: CEREC, 1994).

would be completely useless to ask him what punishment the Indians
deserve, who have utterly destroyed so many Spanish cities around
them, letting almost no creature escape from any of them, burning
and profaning churches, eating the priests, without forgiving 100,000
native Indians the Neiva Valley. Or to ask him to be a judge of the
Indians, as he has been with the conquerors, without wishing to
admit in his defense that, as Plato says, a judge must not sentence nor
determine justice without first hearing both sides; and I am certain
that, hearing them, he would find the Indians just as cruel and bloodthirsty, much more than I claim. And these are not tales of Amadis
that 100,000 or more have died and been weighed in their slaughter-
houses, as public as the ones we have for sheep and cows.

And whoever enters that [upper Magdalena] valley, sixty leagues
long, and ponders such a pleasant land, so full of cattle yet without
owners, as they have all perished, as we have said, and considers the
many towns settled there, by Spaniards and Indians alike, populations in lands rich in deposits of gold and silver, with abundant
resources, hunting and fishing in the rivers, but now sees it abandoned, if this person has reason and understanding he would be
moved to pity, wishing for the opportunity to offer his life to avenge
such destruction and desolation. And so, one need not be surprised
that in the war and punishments that have been pursued, anyone
who is caught is stabbed to death and left in a ravine without a tomb,
and another is hanged and impaled, which are all cruelties that the
Bishop mostly exaggerates and examines. And if this were to happen
to another nation, I believe and hold for certain that they would not
have as much mercy as the Spaniards, for they [the Pijaos] deserve
extraordinary and severe manners of death. And I am certain that
these people will be pacified more quickly with severity rather than
clemency, for this sore is so fistulous that unless strong caustics are
applied, it will become more cancerous; pleasant unguents have no
effect here, as they only serve for newly conquered peoples; and as I
told one [example], I will tell another. I have acted in new conquests
as I did in the provinces of the Andaquíes, where I founded the city
of Simancas, aided by a cacique named Camponay who came out
to receive and seek me with his people, guiding and directing me in
everything.[67] With [people] such as these it is good to be gentle and

---

67. On the establishment and failure of Simancas, see Vargas Machuca, *The Indian
Militia*, 1, 10, 184.

do good works, as well as with those who have been conquered, for [doing] good works is a virtue of generous spirit. But with the Indian who made peace and [swore] obedience to His Majesty and received the Holy Gospel and baptism, and then rebelled with deaths and injuries, there was no lightning bolt quicker to attack than I, even if I had only a few people; for having long experience with them, [I know them to be] like the crocodile or *cayman*, as they are called in the Indies, a relentless pursuer of those who flee, but a fleeing coward to those who boldly pursue and attack it. And with such quickness the land was calmed and made tranquil, and the Indian [made] free; for as St. Augustine says, if he is good, man is free even though he serves.

And I may say and confirm, as a soldier and a Christian, that none of my expeditions have failed because of divine favor, alacrity in punishment and war, and good dealings in [times of] peace; and I believe all commanders do this, for as Seneca says, the spirit is a God and a guest in the human body, and this is understood for all Christians, and this is the reason why they [i.e., the Indians] are often pardoned in [spite of] their rebellion, to see if they make amends. But as an ungrateful people, they fail to recognize this clemency, and it can easily be said that, as St. Chrysostom says, whoever should sin after being pardoned is an ingrate; and in these punishments, justifiably executed by their administrators and encomenderos, they defend [the Indians] as much as possible, and this is easily believed, for the more Indians who die of punishments, the less the estate will have; and it has happened that an encomendero has saved some of them from death one, two, and three times, only to have them give it [i.e., death] to him as thanks. Consider here what the Bishop claims, that the Indians did no evil without having received it first: I would like to know if this retribution is just, that the one[68] who gave them life so many times should die for it. By my account, I find that in the most perverse and cruel nation on earth, nobility is found in saving the captive from whom a notable benefit has been gained, and to this day, nothing like this has ever been seen nor will it ever, and we have great examples of this.

And so as not to tire the reader, let us look at what happened in the province of Santa Marta, and the evil the Indians did to two holy friars, named brother Pedro Montano and brother Francisco de Solís, of the order of St. Augustine. Inflamed by the Holy Spirit, they went

---

68. Or "the master" (*el amo; CDI*, 305).

to preach the Holy Gospel to those [Indians] under their authority, in the churches they had and as they were already Christians. And after a few days, while preaching, they were shot with arrows and martyred, giving up their souls to God. This fine retribution was also found in these people; and no lesser gratitude than this can be found, nor did they ever acknowledge their responsibility. And regarding their nature, I will say that if they should be ordered to work by the intervention of justice, with the proper salary [paid] by a third party or voluntarily, and with only one day left before the sentence is served and they collect their money, and they [see that they] may flee, or it at least crosses their mind, they flee and lose their salary and go quite contentedly to their friends and family, not finishing [work] that day. And other times, they not only choose to lose their salary, but their blankets as well, leaving them behind because they cannot get them back; such is the reason for retaining them by keeping their clothes. In the end, they waste no time if they see [an opportunity], though it may be detrimental to them in some way, like a people possessed by the Devil, from whom nothing good can be expected.

And whenever he decides to make any conquest, every conqueror must not only be prepared for everything, but must do his duty first to God, second, to the King, and third, to himself; for he must enter with the courage to perpetuate himself in the land, founding estates, as any other way would fail; perpetuating oneself requires managing the Indian, for without him, the success and aim behind his making the conquest, as well as sustaining the conquerors, would be gone. For [the Indian] is the true buttress upon which the edifice must be founded, without becoming impassioned or partial, hiding any emulation and ignoring any ill will. We know that the administration of any republic always brings with it certain enmity and hate, and that most times, this makes the commander abandon the settlement and then all is lost. It is also true that it spurs that desire to return to his homeland, to contemplate those steps he took as a boy and the love of his family, with a desire to show how he has become great, which if one considers well the fruits that come of [such experience], one finds that they are quite few, and the risks and dangers are many; and though this appears to be beyond our intention and purpose, it is not, for I mention it in order to persuade every conqueror and settler not to abandon a settlement for these reasons, for in abandoning his settlement, the commander will certainly lose the people and the land that cost him so much work and risk. And we have seen this happen on many and diverse occasions, and as has been said, the fruits of abandoning the town in order to return and strut around the homeland are none; being noble in the homeland, one will be so in the Indies, and if not, it is better to pretend to be so there than in the homeland, unless they should acquire nobility there by the privileges ceded to them because of the conquests.

Believe me, dear conquerors, and keep calm, and conserve what God has given you, and take pleasure in the warmth of the land, of such abundant resources and such wealth; for we may truly say that whoever lives in the Indies may be sure of three things: hunger, poverty, and pestilence; neither Spain nor any other land on earth assures this. Avoid the rigors of the sea and the ill will and infamy that everyone finds upon return; for if he returns wealthy, there is no brother, nephew, family, old friend, or servant, whether they be his own or of someone else, female guests and servant girls, or ministers of justice in any case they come upon, important or not, who do not wish and pretend to participate and share with him all that he brings back; and if he brings much and is generous, there will be so many confidence artists that by the time he notices, he will be poor; and divvied among so many, it will be of little use to them or to him; and I assure you that when this has happened and he should need [his wealth], he will not find it and will be left poor and disliked, for they are all jealous over his giving more to Peter than he did to Paul. And the worst is that being poor now, or returning from the Indies because of some misfortune that has befallen him, no one will believe him nor can he convince them of anything, for they are certain that he walks upon gold, and no matter how many times he swears or gives proof of his poverty, they will say that the returning Spaniards [*Indianos*] are tightfisted and miserly. And this language is so common that in all of Spain there is no man nor woman who does not say this, with no consideration for the poor *Indiano* who has crossed six thousand miles of water with his creed in his mouth [i.e., ready to die] both going and coming; and whether he brings much or little, it has cost him, after a million risks, dangers, and labors, spilling a million drops of blood in wounds and in sweat, such that supporting him and treating him honorably is just, to secure his aims, if he has them, or to live in his homeland. In the courts, I have known many who, returning from the Indies and distributing what they brought, have died miserably, buried with alms; for at this time family members are never found who will take responsibility for his burial. That they died poor because of the gifts they provided I do not dare to say, but it appears to me that the possessions of the *Indianos* have been confiscated by their family connections in Spain.

As an example of all of this, I will relate what a gentleman from Aragon, a friend of mine, told me about what happened to a nobleman of his own kingdom, native of the town of Epila, who, having gone to the Indies and having received from God good fortune and wealth, returned to his land twelve years later. He had the strange idea to enter his town as a broken and destroyed man, pretending to be poor; beneath a miserable habit he carried his great wealth in gold and silver and precious gems, diamonds and others of high value; and he may have had an illness that showed his necessity to test his [people], for he set out for the house of an older brother. Arriving at his door, he declared who he was to a servant girl, and asked that she tell this to his brother who was there at the time. The servant told her master, [describing] the clothes he was wearing and their color, and [the master], who saw him from a window, betrayed him and ordered her to tell him that he was not at home and that he go with God, for he did not recognize him or know who he was. With this answer, he went to the house of another, and was not recognized there either. He had an uncle and remembered to go there, and however it was, he was received with open arms; and his uncle looked at his head to see if he had his ears, and when he saw them he said that he was quite welcome, that since he had his ears [i.e., was not a fugitive criminal], there would be no lack of bread for him in his house as long as he lived. The *Indiano* was so thankful for this that he told him, "God wants my fortune to be yours, for my brothers did not know how to enjoy it. I bring [gifts] for everyone and come in such a manner, that unless God brings a miracle, I will live but a short while." And so it was, that though the uncle gave him all the care he could, he died within a few days, making [his uncle] his inheritor, enjoying his share because of the fine welcome he gave. The brothers were so sorry and so pained because of their misfortune, that I do not wish to ponder it, and I do not name them because of their honor; and they did not regret lacking virtue and brotherhood, but rather not having inherited such a great fortune. This case serves to oblige one to open his eyes and learn from the mistakes of another, as it is wise to do so. In the end, as long as the money lasts, one has friends, but without it, enemies. When a person is in need, whether a father or mother or brothers, I would consider it wise to help as much as one is able, with honor and according to his condition and means; and if one wishes to favor other brothers and relatives, send for them and then favor them, fulfilling his obligation as one is able. And whoever would still return to Spain, unable to avoid it, may he come back rich, very rich, so as to fulfill [his obligations] to all, for if not, he may as well not try, because as Cornelius the Roman [centurion] says, generous hearts are moved to pity by seeing things they cannot remedy.

The tyranny the Spaniards exercise against the Indians in finding or diving for pearls is one of the most cruel and shameful things in the world. There is no hellish and hopeless life on this earth that may be compared with it, however hard and terrible taking out the gold in the mines may be. They throw them into the sea in three and four and five yards' depth from early morning until the sun has set. They are always underwater swimming, without respite, tearing from the seabed the oysters in which the pearls are found.

—Fray Bartolomé de las Casas

The Sixth Discourse and Defense
Regarding the Isle of Margarita.

Furthermore, it seems fitting to me to expand the response to the charges the Bishop makes against the conquerors of the isle of Santo Domingo, the Windward [Islands] and the other places [where] we have been following him throughout all the Western Indies, confronting him with a true and Christian defense, and though it is true that he made no particular charge regarding this isle of Margarita because it was not settled at the time, it would not be out of place to address its settling, exemplary of the Christian behavior that our [people] had there, so that every man with any understanding, and whoever has read or may read his treatise *Destruction of the Indies,* may infer, believe, and be persuaded of how blindly he threw himself into such grave and hateful material.

And beginning our discourse and response, I say that having news of this isle and of the number of the natives that inhabited it, Marcelo de Villalobos resolved to settle it, with powers and title of the Royal Audiencia of Santo Domingo and with soldiers sufficient for its settling; and arriving, they stepped ashore and were warmly received by caciques from every part of the isle, with no sort of war, betrayal, or poor treatment, but rather with great hospitality, affection, and good service.[69] Exploring the island, they settled in the best site they could find at the time, considering the best comforts, with the approval and consent of all. Neither acts of conquest nor the need for punishment

69. Villalobos died upon being named Margarita's first governor in 1525, so his wife, Isabel Manrique, presided until 1535. Members of the Villalobos family governed the island until 1593. See Morella A. Jiménez G., *La esclavitud indígena en Venezuela, siglo XVI* (Caracas: Academia Nacional de la Historia, 1986), 263.

had any place here, for [the Indians] later received the Holy Gospel
and have been baptized to the present day in our holy Catholic faith,
and they will keep [this faith] from now on, without renouncing
what they professed at this time, according to what they have shown
and have given to sustain peace without ever having rebelled nor
retreated from Christian communication.

This isle is at ten degrees [north latitude; really about twelve]
and Santo Domingo is at seventeen [degrees north latitude], with
the distance between them being two hundred leagues, and it is the
last land settled after the isles of Cuba, Jamaica, and Puerto Rico,
and successively New Spain and the provinces of Honduras and
Tierra Firme, the New Kingdom of Granada, the Kingdom of Peru,
Las Charcas, Chile, and the Plate River, and lastly this isle of Margarita, across from Santo Domingo. These [Guayquerí] Indians, of
such a gentle nature, who gave no cause for war nor punishment,
have had unequaled treatment, honor, and freedom in all those days,
and if the others had worked as well, receiving the Holy Gospel and
baptism without committing the betrayals, burnings, and murders
that they always did, they would also [have been treated well]; but
having once made peace only to break it with unheard-of cruelties
and betrayals, it was not right that the Spaniard should allow himself
to be destroyed by them, for self defense is permitted in the entire
universe and necessary so that guilt is offended and punished, as the
Philosopher says. These Indians are the most remarkable, valued,
and privileged; and though it is true that the Tascaltecs [Tlaxcalans]
in New Spain, and those [Indians] of the isle of Puná in Peru, and
the Indians of Vélez in the New Kingdom of Granada welcomed and
aided our [people], they did so for different reasons: finding themselves at war with their neighbors and in need, they welcomed [the
Spaniards] and there was equal correspondence between them. But
among these natives there was no war nor necessity of any aid, and
they were compelled only by good works, from which there have
been almost sixty years of amicable dealings, the Indians respect-
ing our [people] and the Spaniards esteeming them for their good
condition and easy nature in their affairs, although they are such
great warriors and so valiant that the Carib Indians so common
among those islands flee if they catch sight of them. And if at any
time they attacked them or stopped to fight them, they were hand-
ily beaten, which is why they are so feared; and when these [native]

Margariteños, also called Guayqueríes, have attacked the Caribs,
alone or accompanied by Spaniards, they have done incredible deeds,
and as Indians of such great valor they are free from [paying] any
tribute or service, by royal consent, the King honoring them in his
royal letters, where he calls them "my Guayquerí gentlemen," an
honor deserved by their valor and fealty, great, constant, firm, and
proved through long experience.[70] This was particularly noted when
the tyrant Lope de Aguirre took control of the isle and garroted the
governor don Juan de Villalpando and [imposed] similar justice on
the other inhabitants; and those who escaped fled to the countryside
and to the hills, divided, alone or in pairs, and if these [Indian] people
were malicious or had been offended, they would have been able to
finish them all off. This sufficiently dismisses the charge that the
Bishop makes against all the conquerors, of the mistreatment and
cruelties he claims they committed against the natives on the isle of
Hispaniola and the rest of Tierra Firme in all the Indies.[71]

70. The Guayquerí of Margarita were by all accounts early and faithful allies of
the Spanish against neighboring Carib peoples. Though much mixed after five hun-
dred years of sustained contact with outsiders, the Guayquerí are alive and well today.
An early ethnographic study is summarized in W. D. Rosenthal and Thomas McCorkle,
"The Problem of Aboriginal Persistence," *Southwestern Journal of Anthropology* 11:3
(1955): 288–300. On Spanish contact from Columbus's day, see Carl O. Sauer, *The Early
Spanish Main* (Berkeley: University of California Press, 1966), 191. Alexander von
Humboldt described meeting the Guayquerí upon his arrival in Margarita from Spain
on the good ship *Pizarro* in 1799. See Humboldt, *Personal Narrative of a Journey to the
Equinoctial Regions of the New Continent*, trans. Jason Wilson (New York: Penguin,
1995), 47: "In each canoe there were eighteen Guayquerí Indians, naked to the waist
and very tall. They looked very muscular, with a skin color between brown and coppery
red. From afar, sitting still and standing out against the horizon, they could be taken for
bronze statues. Their appearance did not correspond with the traits and extreme weak-
ness described by previous travelers." And on 54: "The word 'Guayquerí,' like the words
'Peru' and 'Peruvian,' owes its origin to a simple mistake. When Christopher Columbus's companions reached Margarita Island, on whose northern tip these Indians still
live, they found several Indians fishing with harpoons, throwing these sharp-pointed
sticks tied with string at the fish. Columbus's men asked the Indians in the Haitian
[Taíno] language what their name was, but the Indians thought the foreigners referred
to their harpoons made of the hard and heavy wood of the macana palm and answered:
'Guaike, guaike,' meaning, 'pointed stick.'"

71. The Aguirre story is well narrated by Stephen Minta, *Aguirre: The Re-creation
of a Sixteenth-Century Journey Across South America* (New York: Henry Holt, 1993),
and some relevant documents may be found in Felix Jay, *Sins, Crimes, and Retribution in Early Latin America: A Translation and Critique of Sources: Lope de Aguirre,
Francisco de Carvajal, and Juan Rodríguez Freyle* (Lewiston, N.Y.: Edwin Mellen Press,
1999).

On the contrary, the kind treatment of these people has been seen, without labor, servitude, nor any such oppression; the Indians are interested only in their comforts and pleasure as if they were Spaniards, freely reaping the benefits of their crops and pearl fisheries, hunting, and other entertainments and ancient customs; but despite this liberty and kind treatment, they have slowly disappeared like the rest of the Indians in all these hot lands, for the number of all these people was once great but today one sees far fewer. And their diminishing implies that within a short time they will have all disappeared completely; the consideration of which should be understood and seen as evidence of divine will, as we have referred to previously in other discussions, serving to empty the Indies of idolatrous peoples in order to populate them with Christians. But as we have proven, in colder lands the [Indian populations] have been conserved by their multiplying when they were distributed into encomiendas, despite the general diseases that have befallen them for some time, greatly reducing their numbers; and in warm lands [these numbers] have decreased rapidly, on the isle of Hispaniola among others, such as this isle of Margarita that we are addressing; and though one appears to contradict the other, absolution has no place in human understanding, being, as it is, reserved only for divine justice. And so I will only say that if the Indians in hot lands die so quickly, it is not nor has it been because of abuse, for we see the contrary in cold lands, and even on this hot island, with all the [kind] treatment and freedom [granted by] the Spaniards, they are dying out, as so happened on Hispaniola and other places with the same climate, and this decrease has been in such a manner that there are no more than 500 people on the entire island, mostly women, children, and the aged, 150 of whom cannot take up arms. But they are such a valiant and bellicose people that with only these few, and though they are divided among ports along their coasts, they defend their settlements from the Carib Indians of Dominica and their allies who so infest the other isles as well as Tierra Firme, such as Santo Domingo, Jamaica, and Puerto Rico, Trinidad and also the coast of Tierra Firme from the Lapure River up to the Cape of San Román, by a distance of more than four hundred leagues, east to west, where a million natives have disappeared (and if one said two million it would not be an exaggeration). This [loss caused by the Caribs occurred] in the past as well as the present, with many burnings, robberies, and incredible deaths with unheard-of

cruelties. The Bishop should call these [Caribs] cruel tyrants, with
no mercy or clemency, by whose hands a great number of Spaniards have suffered and died, both males and females, none escaping
because of age or condition; burning and razing many towns and
farms with livestock, sugar mills and, in the ports, a great number of
ships loaded with merchandise from Spain and the Indies and blacks
from Guinea, decimating the people who sailed them and sail them
today, with neither the French, the English, nor the Flemish [i.e.,
Dutch] escaping. These Indians who create so much havoc and cause
so much harm, what moves them to it? Up to now, the Spaniards
have not set foot upon their lands, nor settled nor even attempted
conquest, a thing that would be quite important for the service of
God and the King, conquering and settling these islands for the
security of all the lands referred to, as well as [the safety] of every
ship that suffers along these coasts and ports, as well as those arriving, a concern for the fleets and convoys that sail to New Spain and
Tierra Firme when they arrive to take on water; few escape without
their people being captured and taken away, a great misfortune. This
[example] of the pitiless nature of the Indians will be sufficient to
contradict the Bishop when he wrote of their generally good [nature]
in all of the Western Indies and in particular, those of the isle of
Hispaniola, at least ten leagues away from those of Dominica and the
other confederate [i.e., Carib-dominated] isles, where the proof would
be in going to preach the Gospel to them without the fearsome presence of the soldiers, as he says. I believe and hold it for certain that he
would not make it out alive and that the fruits of his labors would be
but few, if any, because of their evil nature; and if he managed to do
well among those of the isle of Margarita, Tascala [Tlaxcala], Puná,
and Vélez, it was granted by Heaven, from whence came [the conces-
sion] of the Royal Majesty and the kind treatment and reciprocity
of the settlers; and if others in the Indies had [this concession], it
would have been for the same reasons, for good works are bound by
the heart.

When God wished to bestow upon these Indians of Margarita the
aforementioned condition, He gave them many earthly goods surrounding their houses and island, these being the oriental pearls, the
most noble among human riches, pleasant and coveted, their benefit
[received] with neither labor nor expense, for from the moment
they are taken from the sea they are [already] molded, carved, and

finished, unlike other valuable items such as gold, silver, and precious stones; this happy poultice for the heart is valued more than others by all nations, as it has the highest price and the least volume. God wished to give this seed, so unusual and excellent, to these Indians more than to any others in all the Indies; the creation of these *margaritas* [seed pearls] reveals and demonstrates a remarkable philosophy, something that, even though it is unrelated to our purpose here, should be permitted simply for the pleasure of understanding it.

Thus, in order to create these precious pearls, we will say that four conditions must be perfectly met, and that if any one of them is not met, the generation of this seed cannot take place. The first is the disposition of the sea floor, being either sand or rock [*peña* (in this case, coral)], which must continue uninterrupted at the same depth, or being at a depth from four to twelve arm-lengths, so that the oysters do not roll with the tidal currents when they mature and release themselves from their beds; [here,] the influence of the rays from the sun penetrate and reach them with effect, something they cannot do [at a depth of] twelve or deeper, as long experience has shown; neither can they be grown between the depths of four [arm-lengths] and the shore, and if [there are] any, they are but few, because of the tumbling of the undercurrents and tides, which prevent their growth, which is why they are moved to a depth between four and twelve arm-lengths. The second condition for their creation is that there be dew from the heavens and some rain that lends the seed its sensitive soul. The third is that they have the spawning or feeding grounds necessary for their alimentation with a vegetative soul, until the oyster reaches the stage for creating pearls. The fourth is that the land be hot and within the confines of the sun and at the latitude whereby the rays strike perpendicularly twice a year; and the rest [of the year], the [angle of the rays] should not be so oblique that they do not have any effect, even though the land may be ten or twenty degrees north or south [latitude], as known by experience. Up to ten [degrees] of latitude they grow with greater strength and brevity and are more oriental [i.e., of higher quality]; and if they grow in cold lands, even though the other conditions are met and some are grown, they will be flawed [*abromadas*, literally, "worm-eaten"] and of little value, as has been observed along the coasts near the two tropics, either within them or outside of them, such that the lower the latitude at which they are found, the more oriental they are, as long as they are not grown in mud. On rock or in sand, their brilliance [*oriente*] will be assured, such as those from this island, which lies at twenty degrees north, more or less, as do the other surrounding isles of Coche and Cubagua and Río de la Hacha [Riohacha, Colombia, on the mainland], where the four conditions are met. These pearls die from the fresh waters of the rivers and their currents, as experience has shown, and they are not found where rivers enter the sea, and where they might be found would be a land completely devoid of them along the entire coast from one end to another. And taking this philosophy further, I find that they do not die because of the fresh water and its currents, so much as due to the turbulence in the floods; the oyster has such a delicate and pure nature that any mud or bad odor kills them, as has already been observed. In the end, with such a precious fruit, what could one expect from a climate that created the beauty of these *margaritas* and a soil that produces them along all her coasts, but that the land be the healthiest of all the Indies, as such it is, and that the Indians be so valiant and well blessed, gentle, and of such an admirable condition?

VOCABULARY OF TERMS IN THIS TREATISE

A

APO is a supreme lord.

ARCABUCOS are thick forests or jungles.

AMBIRE is an herb [*contrahierba, Dorstenia contrajerva L.*] and compound against all venoms, generally.

AMAHAGUA is the bark of a tree that can be used like hemp.

B

BARBACOA is [made of] four forked stakes stuck into the earth, supporting a platform of sticks or canes, used to sleep upon, as well as to cook and smoke meat or fish by making a fire beneath.

BIHAO is a tree leaf almost as large as a shield and quite useful.

BIJA is a turpentine made with a color called *bija* or *achote* [*achiote, Bixa orellana L.*], which is similar to henna, with which the Indian paints himself to become more ferocious.

C

CACIQUE is what could be considered a lord with vassals.

ÇABANA is a land cleared of trees, abundant in grass such as a pasture or meadow, long grass if it is in a hot land.

CAMAS is a type of platform made of thick canes, called *guadicas* [probably *Guadua angustifolia*] in those places, and in some provinces the Indians sleep upon them.

CEYBA [Ceiba] is a very large tree; there are two types, one is covered in thorns and the other is without them; the thorny [type] produces a milk that is used to make deadly venom, and is also used to kill fish in the rivers, making them drunk with it.

G

GUAZABARA is the same as battle.

GUAGUA is the fruit of a tree, the juice of which is used by the Indians to paint themselves a black color that does not come off for nine days.

H

CHASQUES [fr. Quechua *chasqui*] are foot messengers.

HAMACA is a net made of cotton-thread fabric or of reeds, hung in the air from wall to wall or from tree to tree, and slept in.

HIGUERON is a tree with a very light wood similar to cork.

CHACARA [fr. Quechua *chagra*] is a garden.

M

MOHAN is, for heathens, a prophet, but among us [Christians] and in truth, a sorcerer or fortune-teller.

MACANA is an arm wielded by the Indians like a longsword.

MAZATO is a drink [made] of sour corn mash.

P

PIRAGUAS are as if we were to say long and narrow boats made of one tree-trunk or of two.

PAMPANILLA is a cotton cloth with which the Indian men and women cover their dishonest parts.

T

TAMBO is an uninhabited house in a village or the country, where travelers stay.

TOTUMA is what we can imagine [to be] half of a round gourd, though of a different type and larger, from which the Indian eats and drinks, lacking any other thing for such a purpose.

Y

YANACONA is a page or manual servant for the Spaniard.

YUCA [manioc] is a useful root, of which a bread is made and eaten called *cazabe*.

I have seen this treatise entitled *Defense and Discourse of the Western Conquests,* composed by don Bernardo de Vargas Machuca, and do not find within it anything against our Holy Catholic Faith or good customs, rather [finding it] favorable to his God and Catholic Majesty, the author showing much Christian zeal and the loyalty of a vassal to our king. Therefore, it seems to me that it may be printed. In San Felipe, Madrid, July 20 of the year 1618.

Don Manuel de Villegas Peralta

Adorno, Rolena. *The Polemics of Possession in Spanish American Narrative.* New Haven: Yale University Press, 2007.

Bakewell, Peter. "Conquest After the Conquest: The Rise of Spanish Domination in America." In *Spain, Europe, and the Atlantic World: Essays in Honour of John H. Elliott,* ed. Richard Kagan and Geoffrey Parker, 296–315. New York: Cambridge University Press, 1995.

Bataillon, Marcel. *Études sur Bartolomé de las Casas.* Paris: Centre de recherches de l'Institut d'études hispaniques, 1965.

Bolaños, Alvaro Félix. *Barbarie y canibalismo en la retórica colonial de los indios Pijaos de Fray Pedro Simón.* Bogotá: CEREC, 1994.

Bushnell, David. *El Libertador: Writings of Simón Bolívar.* Trans. Frederick Fornoff. New York: Oxford University Press, 2003.

Castro, Daniel. *Another Face of Empire: Bartolomé de las Casas, Indigenous Rights, and Ecclesiastical Imperialism.* Durham: Duke University Press, 2007.

Clendinnen, Inga. "'Fierce and Unnatural Cruelty': Cortés and the Conquest of Mexico." *Representations,* 33 (Winter 1991): 65–100.

Díaz del Castillo, Bernal. *The History of the Conquest of New Spain.* Ed. Davíd Carrasco. Trans. A. P. Maudslay. Albuquerque: University of New Mexico Press, 2008.

Dillehay, Tom D. *Monuments, Empires, and Resistance: The Araucanian Polity and Ritual Narratives.* New York: Cambridge University Press, 2007.

Flores Hernández, Benjamín. "Pelear con el Cid después de muerto: Las *Apologías y discursos de las conquistas occidentales* de Bernardo de Vargas Machuca, en controversia con la *Brevísima relación de la destrucción de las Indias* de Fray Bartolomé de las Casas." In *Estudios de Historia Novohispana* X, 45–105. Mexico City: UNAM, 1991.

———. "Bernardo de Vargas Machuca y el Caribe." *Revista Mexicana del Caribe* 14 (2002): 81–103.

Francis, J. Michael, ed. *Invading Colombia: Spanish Accounts of the Gonzalo Jiménez de Quesada Expedition of Conquest.* University Park: Pennsylvania State University Press, 2007.

Friede, Juan, and Benjamin Keen, eds. *Bartolomé de las Casas in History: Toward an Understanding of the Man and His Work.* DeKalb: Northern Illinois University Press, 1971.

Hanke, Lewis. *The Spanish Struggle for Justice in the Conquest of America.* Philadelphia: University of Pennsylvania Press, 1949.

———. *Bartolomé de las Casas: An Interpretation of His Life and Writings.* The Hague: Martinus Nijhoff, 1951.

———. *Bartolomé de las Casas, Historian: An Essay in Spanish Historiography.* Gainesville: University of Florida Press, 1952.

———. "The Meaning Today of the Las Casas Treatises Published in 1552." In *Selected Writings of Lewis Hanke on the History of Latin America,* 96–102. Tempe: ASU Center for Latin American Studies, 1979.

———. "More Heat and Some Light on the Spanish Struggle for Justice in the Conquest of America." *Hispanic American Historical Review* 44 (1964): 293–340. Reprinted in *Selected Writings of Lewis Hanke on the History of Latin America,* 26–48. Tempe: ASU Center for Latin American Studies, 1979.

Hanke, Lewis, and Manuel Giménez Fernández. *Bartolomé de las Casas, 1474–1566: Bibliografía crítica y cuerpo de materiales para el estudio de su vida, escritos, actuación y polémicas que suscitaron durante cuatro siglos.* Santiago de Chile: Fondo Histórico y Bibliográfico José Toribio Medina, 1954.

Hemming, John. *The Conquest of the Incas.* New York: Harcourt Brace, 1970.

Humboldt, Alexander von. *Personal Narrative of a Journey to the Equinoctial Regions of the New Continent.* Abridged. Trans. Jason Wilson. New York: Penguin, 1995.

Jopling, Carol F., ed. *Indios y negros en Panamá en los Siglos XVI y XVII: Selecciones de los documentos del Archivo General de Indias.* South Woodstock, Vt.: Plumsock Mesoamerican Studies, 1994.

Keith Nauman, Ann. *The Career of Doña Inés de Suárez, the First European Woman in Chile.* Lewiston, N.Y.: Edwin Mellen, 2000.

Lane, Kris. *Colour of Paradise: The Emerald in the Age of Gunpowder Empires.* New Haven: Yale University Press, 2010.

———. *Quito 1599: City and Colony in Transition.* Albuquerque: University of New Mexico Press, 2002.

Las Casas, Bartolomé de. *An Account, Much Abbreviated, of the Destruction of the Indies.* Ed. Franklin Knight. Trans. Andrew Hurley. Indianapolis: Hackett Publishing, 2003.

———. *In Defense of the Indians.* Trans. and ed. Stafford Poole. DeKalb: Northern Illinois University Press, 1974. (Orig. composed ca. 1550.)

———. *Tratados.* Ed. Lewis Hanke and Manuel Giménez Fernández. Trans. Agustín Millares Carlo and Rafael Moreno. Mexico: Fondo de Cultura Económica, 1965.

———. *Historia de las Indias.* 3 vols. Mexico City: FCE, 1951.

———. *Apologética historia sumaria.* Ed. Edmundo O'Gorman. 2 vols. Mexico City: UNAM, 1967.

Las Casas, Bartolomé de. *La destrucción de las Indias* and *Refutación de Las Casas*. Ed. Juan Guixé. Paris: Biblioteca económica de clásicos castellanos, 1913 [?].

Maltby, William S. *The Black Legend in England: The Development of Anti-Spanish Sentiment, 1558–1660.* Durham: Duke University Press, 1971.

Martínez de Salinas, María Luisa. *Castilla ante el Nuevo Mundo: La trayectoria indiana del gobernador Bernardo de Vargas Machuca.* Valladolid, Spain: Diputación Provincial, 1991.

Menéndez Pidal, Ramón. *Bartolomé de Las Casas: Su doble personalidad.* Madrid: Espasa-Calpe, 1963.

Muldoon, James. *The Americas in the Spanish World Order: The Justification for Conquest in the Seventeenth Century.* Philadelphia: University of Pennsylvania Press, 1994.

Padden, Robert C. "Cultural Adaptation and Militant Autonomy Among the Araucanians of Chile." *Southwestern Journal of Anthropology* 13:1 (Spring 1957): 103–21.

Restall, Matthew. *Seven Myths of the Spanish Conquest.* New York: Oxford University Press, 2003.

Restall, Matthew, and Florine Asselbergs. *Invading Guatemala: Spanish, Nahua, and Maya Accounts of the Conquest Wars.* University Park: Pennsylvania State University Press, 2007.

Sarmiento de Gamboa, Pedro. *History of the Incas.* Ed. and trans. Brian S. Bauer and Vania Smith. Austin: University of Texas Press, 2007.

Sauer, Carl O. *The Early Spanish Main.* Berkeley: University of California Press, 1966.

Schmidt-Nowara, Christopher. *The Conquest of History: Spanish Colonialism and National Histories in the Nineteenth Century.* Pittsburgh: University of Pittsburgh Press, 2006.

Stabler, Arthur P., and John E. Kicza. "Ruy González's 1553 Letter to Emperor Charles V: An Annotated Translation." *The Americas* 42:4 (April 1986): 473–87.

van Groesen, Michiel. *The Representations of the Overseas World in the De Bry Collection of Voyages (1590–1634).* Leiden: Brill, 2008.

Vargas Machuca, Bernardo de. *The Indian Militia and Description of the Indies.* Ed. Kris Lane. Trans. Timothy F. Johnson. Durham: Duke University Press, 2008.

———. *Michi no senshi to no takakai.* Trans. Aoki Yasuyuki. Tokyo: Iwanami Shoten, 1994.

———. *Apologías y discursos de las conquistas occidentales.* Ed. and trans. María Luisa Martínez de Salinas. Ávila, Spain: Junta de Castilla y León, 1993. (From orig. Salamanca manuscript, 1618.)

———. "Apologías y discursos de las Conquistas Occidentales." In *Colección de documentos inéditos para las historia de España,* ed. José Sancho Rayón and Francisco de Zabalburu, 71:201–309. Madrid: Miguel Ginesta, 1879. (From orig. Salamanca manuscript, 1618.)

Wagner, Henry R., and Helen R. Parish. *The Life and Writings of Bartolomé de las Casas.* Albuquerque: University of New Mexico Press, 1967.

Wey Gómez, Nicolás. *Tropics of Empire: Why Columbus Sailed South to the Indies.* Cambridge, Mass.: MIT Press, 2008.

Whitehead, Neil L., ed. *Wolves from the Sea: Readings in the Anthropology of the Native Caribbean.* Leiden: KITLV, 1995.

latin american originals

Titles in print